PRAISE FOR *THE CHUBBY*

"Justin and Amy bring huge flavor and modern style to easy and unexpected vegetarian recipes, perfect for chic entertaining — or any night of the week."

– **Lloyd Boston:** TV host, author, and Style Contributor known to millions of viewers as Style Contributor on NBC's *Today Show* and expert guest on *Oprah*, ABC's *The View*, *The Insider*, *Extra*, *Access Hollywood*, and *The Wendy Williams Show*.

"I love Justin and Amy's creativity in each and every dish. They take common vegetables and transform them into beautiful and tasty treats. Each recipe photo draws me in to want to take a bite."

– **Whitney Miller:** Season 1 *MasterChef* winner, chef at The COOP, and author of *Whitney Miller's New Southern Table*.

"*The Chubby Vegetarian* offers mouthwatering recipes that even lifelong 'I will never eat rabbit food' omnivores will find irresistible. From their take on classic American comfort foods (see the ingenious 'Charred Carrot Hot Dogs') to their renditions of regional mainstays from around the globe ('Masala Dosa' for the win), Justin and Amy further demystify plant-centered, from-scratch cooking in this informative and approachable book."

– **Bryant Terry,** James Beard Foundation Leadership Award-winning chef and author of *Afro-Vegan* and *Vegan Soul Kitchen*.

"I love keeping an eye on what Justin and Amy are doing — it's never less than fascinating and always inspiring."

– **Amanda Cohen:** Chef-owner of Dirt Candy, an all-vegetable restaurant located in New York City's East Village and recommended by the Michelin Guide, and author of *Dirt Candy: A Cookbook*.

"I really love what Justin and Amy are doing: a really bold approach to veg cooking."

– **Rich Landau:** Chef and co-owner of Vedge and V Street and co-author of *Vedge: 100 Plates Both Large and Small that Redefine Vegetable Cooking*.

"I have to write this quickly, because I have almond flour biscuits in the oven, beets curing in pastrami spices, and spaghetti squash slices on the grill: Friends are coming for dinner, and I'm making a raft of colorful, bold recipes from Justin and Amy's mesmerizing new book. Who knew vegetables could be this enticing, this worldly? They did — and now everyone else does, too."

– **Joe Yonan:** *Food and Dining* Editor, *The Washington Post*, and author of *Eat Your Vegetables*.

THE CHUBBY VEGETARIAN

100 INSPIRED VEGETABLE RECIPES FOR THE MODERN TABLE

JUSTIN FOX BURKS & AMY LAWRENCE

SUSAN SCHADT PRESS

We dedicate this cookbook to all of the readers who have kept up with our blog throughout the years. To the people who have given us chances that we never dreamed we would have. And to the friends and family members who love us and our cooking beyond measure. We feel so much gratitude for all the folks in Memphis and throughout the country who have believed in our mission from the very beginning.

CONTENTS

· ·

P. ALLEN SMITH

It's no accident many fruits and vegetables begin their lives as flowers. They bud and bloom, grow tall or sprawl, and then transform into peppers or squash or tomatoes. Watching this transformation is my favorite part of the growing season.

As a child, I would spend hours in the garden, watching the blooms become tiny green morsels, which would ripen into juicy tomatoes, watermelons, or cucumbers. My other favorite part of the season is when those outrageously large yellow crookneck squash plants started to produce. I couldn't wait until my mother turned the harvest into one of my favorite summer dishes: fried squash and okra. I've always felt such gratitude for plants, which take nutrients from the earth and air and turn them into something that is first beautiful and delicate, and then all at once healthy and delicious. Those vegetables, in turn, nourish our bodies, and we also become healthy and productive.

In order for this system to work, edibles need our time and attention to grow. A large harvest of edibles does not come easily. It takes planning and weeding and troubleshooting. We are given a lesson from this, too: we learn to find beauty in the toil. The hard work begets appreciation. That appreciation goes both ways, from seedling to sower and back again. Plants working hard to produce edibles should be appreciated for their efforts, and I believe the best way to appreciate them is to allow them to transform again—into beautiful meals. And no one appreciates them better in that way than the Chubby Vegetarian. The recipes and photographs in this book are equal parts mouthwatering and stunning. These two truly honor the vegetables and their flavors, allowing them to shine in everyday dishes in unexpected ways. I'm consistently inspired by their creativity and resourcefulness in the kitchen.

It's my pleasure to know them and to inspire them in return.

P. Allen Smith is an award-winning designer and gardening and lifestyle expert, providing ideas and inspiration through multiple platforms including broadcast, print, and new media.

INTRODUCTION

LOOKING OUT & LOOKING IN

BY JUSTIN FOX BURKS & AMY LAWRENCE

Though we didn't officially meet each other until an assigned locker was switched in a sly and crafty fashion during the 1990-1991 school year, we have a shared history in many ways. We were both born in small towns in Mississippi, and when we were little, our families moved from Jackson and Greenwood to a suburb right outside of Memphis, Tennessee.

We both grew up in Germantown, where we sat down to dinner with our respective families for some pretty traditional Southern meat-and-three meals like fried chicken or steak with a side of green beans, a baked potato, cucumber and tomato salad, or mac and cheese. That is until the unlikely idea to become a vegetarian came simultaneously to many kids in and around Memphis; both of us were swept up by the trend as well. Maybe it was rebellion, or maybe we had all gotten tired of barbecue—it's hard to say exactly what incited this movement. All of a sudden in our town, it just became really cool to not eat meat. Just the simple introduction of this idea made our plates much more exciting. By the time we'd met, we'd both already gone from looking only at our longstanding Southern ways to peering outward at culinary traditions from all over the globe.

It wasn't long before we were eating foods that we'd never even heard about and also paying closer attention to ingredients and flavors. The first time one of us made falafel from a box mix he acquired from the 'International' section of the supermarket, he pronounced it phonetically: *fal-a-fill*. He'd mash it into the shape of a hamburger patty and serve it on a bun. At the same point in time, the other one, along with her suddenly vegan little sister, was preparing some alien ingredient called tofu by marinating it and stuffing it into sandwiches in place of cold cuts. Both of us got some questioning glances from anyone over the age of 25.

In our teens and twenties, we were falling in love with each other, and soon the lines of our lives that had once paralleled started to converge. We were already both curious and adventurous eaters who craved the story behind a dish as much as the food on the plate. On our early dates, we sought out natural foods restaurants, of which surprisingly, there were quite a few in Memphis in the '90s.

During college here in town, we branched out from our usual pasta-or-sandwich routine. We expanded our repertoire and started reading cookbooks together and making spanikopita, stir-fry, lasagna, dragon bowls, and curries for a crowd of English majors and art school friends. Maybe it was our egos being lifted by the way everyone loved our first attempts at grown-up cooking, or maybe it's just that college students can always eat, eat, and then eat more.

For us, food and cooking had evolved to become a way that we participated in a larger discussion. It became the way we made the odd new surroundings of dorm rooms, apartments, and rental homes feel more welcoming. It was a creative outlet that provided instant gratification. It became the way we took care of each other and the people around us, and it felt great.

It wasn't all wonderful, though, since our love of food eventually led us down a less-than-healthy road. We could figure out how to make anything we wanted at any time, and while it was a blast, well, we both gained weight...and not a little. Our mamas still loved us, and our friends still came over for dinner. This wasn't about our self-worth. It was purely a health issue, and we were determined to conquer it.

Facing this type of change was pretty uncomfortable and overwhelming. All of a sudden, we found ourselves having to re-think everything we felt we knew about food and being vegetarian. We didn't want to give up fun meals with friends, holiday favorites with the family, or a really good dinner every night at home. We were forced to figure out how to eat in a way that bolstered our health instead of chipping away at it day by day. And if we were going to continue to eat a vegetarian diet, we definitely had to focus more on vegetables rather than only focusing on being meatless.

As we both approached 40, we often thought about who we'd like to be years later. And as we've slowly come to realize, there are some simple things that will make the path easier: the right food and the proper amount of it, along with exercise every day and some treats here and there. As simple as it sounds, it works. Some days are less than stellar, and sometimes we need a re-boot in order to get back on track.

Early on, *The Chubby Vegetarian* blog was created as a way for us to visually document the new dishes that were coming out of our kitchen. The name was all about our love of food; it was a joke at first and self-deprecating in a silly, knowing way. On June 29th, 2008, we posted for the first time: a photo of 'Homemade Roasted Corn Sopes with Pumpkin Seeds and Smoky Salsa.' After we'd just been posting photos, readers started asking us how to make the meals we shared online, so we learned how to write recipes. When *The Chubby Vegetarian* was named a Blog of Note by *Blogspot*, we thought we might be on to something, and we decided to see where it took us.

Soon, we began writing for local publications as well as for our blog, and we interviewed chefs, reviewed restaurants, and compiled essays about our experience cooking and our experiments with new ingredients. In 2013, our first cookbook, *The Southern Vegetarian: 100 Down-Home Recipes for the Modern Table*, was published, and it led us to new opportunities. We got to present our ideas and recipes for a vegetarian Thanksgiving meal for the *Well* blog

of *The New York Times*. Next, we were over the moon to be invited to share our unique perspective and cook three dishes as invited guests at the James Beard House in New York City as a part of their 'Enlightened Eaters' series.

In all that we do, our vision has always been to help others love nutritious food and enjoy cooking at home. We are so grateful to everyone who gave us a chance to get our perspective out into the world, the people who believed in what we were doing and opened up channels that allowed our ideas to thrive.

These days, we think differently about how vegetables can be served. They need not be only a side dish or an afterthought. Vegetables can be amazing if we all do one thing: treat them like a piece of meat. We char carrots, stuff them into hot dog buns, and top them with chili, or we bake them into a gratin of sorts and serve them with dill and crème fraîche in a dish reminiscent of a smoked salmon appetizer. We roast eggplants until they pull apart like pork or grill them and layer them into bánh mì sandwiches alongside cilantro, pickled carrots and radishes, and mushroom paté. In our hands, cauliflower can become hot wings or a steak. It's really how you prep and cook the ingredient that makes for an awesome dish.

Cooking is a way to bring order to a chaotic world, and putting more meals together at home has some wonderful and surprising effects. However, keep in mind that striving for perfection is not necessary. We believe it's also important not to stress out too much about the purity, beauty, and ideal nature of every meal. Do what you can each week as you gather ingredients in a way that works for you, but remind yourself, like we always do, that the main goal is preparing meals that come together easily as you utilize the time and the resources that you have at the moment. And if you happen to have a few doubters in your life, and you just *know* they're going to balk at a vegetarian meal, we have some advice for that, too: just play down what you're cooking and let the food on the table do the convincing for you. In other words, make good food that just *happens* to be vegetarian.

Whether we're quizzing the friendly guy at the Indian grocery store about how to make dosas or getting our friends to write down all the secrets of Thai noodle bowls, we are infinitely curious about new flavors and dishes. We figured out the best presentation of these dishes and their just-right flavor profiles over time so we could confidently share them with you. In addition, inspiration rather than strict adherence to authenticity is the most important trait of each of our recipes. We're always up for the challenge of creating a dish that may not be 100% authentic to its roots, but one that stands as our interpretation of it as people who love vegetables. These dishes are our creative translations, and they represent the regular rotation of international cuisines at our house each week.

We believe that your plate, almost more than anything else, speaks volumes about who you are, where you come from, what you hope for, your values, and your ethics. Each plate is your own canvas to share with whomever you choose. These recipes are for you, the home cook, and for those who are ready to see how vegetables can lead us all to feel lighter and more energetic. Come along with us through these chapters and see what these recipes can do in your life and your kitchen.

– **JUSTIN** & **AMY**

ESSENTIAL KITCHEN TOOLS

. . . .

When our dishwasher flooded underneath ceramic tile, we had to have the kitchen and the adjoining dining room completely gutted and rebuilt. We took the opportunity to design the work space of our dreams, which was so much fun. We also had to reorganize every drawer and cabinet and figure out what we really needed to have on hand and what could be stored outside of the kitchen. The following stuff is what made the cut.

The first thing to invest in before anything else on the list is this: *a good, sharp knife.*

We love our Global® 8-inch chef's knife. We also use a Hammer Stahl® knife set. Just be sure to take care of your good knives by carefully rinsing them with warm soapy water and wiping them clean with a kitchen towel. We store our set in a knife block in a drawer. We also have a few colorful ceramic knives in regular rotation, and those can be put in the dishwasher and be just fine.

BASIC ITEMS

Stainless steel mixing bowls, silicone spatulas, whisks of all sizes, metal spatulas, a cheese grater, colanders, a spider or mesh strainer, small prep bowls, glass food storage containers, heat-safe trivets, a set of stainless steel measuring cups and measuring spoons, a liquid measuring cup (clear glass with measurements on the side), metal kitchen tongs, microplanes, cutting boards (wood, plastic, and silicone), bench scraper, large and small spring-action ice cream scoops, regular and serrated peelers, parchment paper

SMALL APPLIANCES

A good-quality food processor, a well-constructed, mostly metal blender, an immersion blender, outdoor grill

POTS AND PANS

3-quart saucepan with lid, 8-quart stockpot, 10-inch and 12-inch frying pans, 17 x 12-inch rimmed baking sheets, cast-iron grill pan

(There are some other special tools we use only for specific dishes; you will see any special equipment listed with the recipes in this book.)

THE WELL-STOCKED VEGETARIAN PANTRY

· ·

We like to be sure we're always able to cook something great using the stuff we already have at home, so a well-stocked pantry is essential. Many of the following ingredients are essential to have on hand in your cupboard and fridge.

FATS
Olive oil, coconut oil, unsalted butter, vegan margarine (if we're cooking for our vegan friends)

FLOURS AND STARCHES
Sprouted wheat flour, all-purpose flour, yellow corn grits, cornmeal, bread crumbs

RICE AND PASTA
Long-grain brown rice, jasmine rice, spaghetti noodles, penne

NUTS
Almonds (sliced and whole), pecans, walnuts, roasted peanuts, pine nuts, peanut butter, almond butter, chocolate hazelnut butter

BEANS
Black beans, refried beans, pinto beans, black-eyed peas, chickpeas, cannellini beans, lentils (especially the brown and red varieties)

SWEETENERS
Maple syrup, honey, sorghum, raw cane sugar, light brown sugar, powdered sugar, dates

SAUCES AND CONDIMENTS
Hickory Smoked Hot Sauce (page 253), sambal, sriracha, Tabasco®, Valentina® Hot Sauce, tomato paste, Zatarain's® Creole mustard, Bragg® Liquid Aminos, organic ketchup, olive oil mayonnaise, vegetarian Worcestershire sauce, liquid smoke

MILK AND CREAM
Whole milk, almond milk, heavy whipping cream

VINEGAR
White vinegar, rice vinegar, champagne vinegar, sherry vinegar, balsamic vinegar, apple cider vinegar

SPICES
Thyme, dill, paprika, smoked paprika, Italian seasoning, coriander seed, ground coriander, cumin, rubbed sage, garlic powder, red pepper flakes, ancho chili powder, clove, nutmeg, cinnamon, ginger, cayenne, chipotle, allspice, curry, Old Bay®, cream of tartar, vanilla extract, vanilla beans, vanilla powder

SALT AND PEPPER
Kosher salt, Maldon® sea salt flakes, hickory smoked sea salt, Tellicherry black peppercorns (for the grinder)

PRODUCE
Garlic, shallots, celery, carrots, flat-leaf parsley, thyme, cilantro, basil, sweet potatoes, Yukon Gold potatoes, sweet onions, lemons, limes, oranges, Pink Lady and Granny Smith apples, bananas, berries, tomatoes, avocados

OTHER ITEMS
Canned tomatoes, tortillas, vegetarian stock or broth in a box, vegetarian bouillon cubes, cooking wine (like Pinot Grigio), mirin, oats, rapid-rise yeast, baking soda, baking powder

BREAKFAST

· ·

OAT, BANANA, AND CHIA SILVER DOLLAR PANCAKES

We always make pancakes on the weekend! There's not much tradition going on otherwise at our house because that's so boring, but we stick to this one. With these for breakfast, you work in a few nutritious ingredients (chia, oats, coconut oil, berries), and with that good of a start, you can just eat whatever you like later on in the day. They're gluten-free, and they're delicious, an amazing combination.

Makes 1 dozen; serves 2.

- 1 CUP ROLLED OATS
- 2 LARGE EGGS
- 1 RIPE BANANA
- 1 TABLESPOON CHIA SEEDS
- 1 TEASPOON BAKING POWDER

- 1 TEASPOON VANILLA
- 1 TABLESPOON COCONUT OIL (MORE FOR COOKING)
- 1/4 CUP MILK (ALMOND, SOY, OR DAIRY)
- 1/2 TEASPOON KOSHER SALT

- BERRIES, BANANAS, AND HONEY OR MAPLE SYRUP (TO SERVE)

Heat a large cast-iron skillet or large, non-stick frying pan over medium-low heat. Into the work bowl of your food processor, place the oats and grind them into a fine flour. Add the eggs, banana, chia, baking powder, vanilla, coconut oil, milk, and salt and blend until smooth. (Unlike traditional flours, you really can't overwork this batter because there's no gluten to activate.) The mixture should be thick but pourable like a traditional pancake batter. Add more milk if needed.

Place about 1 teaspoon of coconut oil on the griddle and brush to coat. Place 1/8 cup of batter on the griddle. It should expand into a 2-inch circle. Repeat. Allow pancakes to cook for 4 minutes or until bubbles start to form on the surface and the underside is golden. Carefully flip the pancakes and cook for another 3 minutes or until each pancake is golden and set all the way through. Repeat until all the batter is used. Serve warm with a drizzle of honey or maple syrup, bananas, and berries.

SALSA-POACHED EGGS

Poaching eggs in tomato sauce or salsa not only saves fat and calories compared to frying, but it also imparts great flavor into the eggs during the cooking process. As a bonus, it couldn't be simpler. We use this method all the time! All you have to do is heat the sauce in a shallow pan and drop the eggs into it. Once the whites are set, they're done.

This recipe is quick enough to make before school or work, but it's also delicious for Sunday brunch with a side of roasted sweet potatoes. It makes for a great, quick dinner if you add a side of black beans and rice and a little queso fresco. Once you try it, we're fairly sure you'll make this again and again.

Serves 2.

- 1 MEDIUM JALAPEÑO PEPPER
- 2 MEDIUM TOMATOES (CORED)
- 1 CLOVE GARLIC
- 1 TEASPOON CHAMPAGNE VINEGAR

- 1/2 TEASPOON KOSHER SALT
- 4 LARGE EGGS
- 1 LARGE WHOLE-WHEAT TORTILLA
- 1 MEDIUM AVOCADO (PEELED, SEEDED, AND SLICED)

- SOUR CREAM, CHIVES, KOSHER SALT, AND CRACKED BLACK PEPPER (TO GARNISH)

Into the work bowl of your food processor, add the jalapeño, tomatoes, garlic, vinegar, and salt. Pulse until everything is broken down but not liquified. Transfer contents to a 8-inch frying pan and set over medium heat. Once the salsa starts bubbling, crack the eggs into the pan while leaving space between them.

While the eggs are cooking, cut the tortilla into three triangles and place two triangles into the toaster. Reserve the other for another use. Place a toasted tortilla on each of the plates. Top with sliced avocado. Once the whites in the eggs have set (about 8 minutes), top each avocado with two eggs and half of the warm salsa. Garnish with a dollop of sour cream and a sprinkling of chives. Add salt and pepper to taste.

AMAZING ALMOND FLOUR BISCUITS

Making up our own gluten-free recipes has certainly been an amazing journey and a life-changing experience, all very similar to how it must feel to be a contestant on *The Bachelor* or *The Bachelorette*. Let's continue this lofty analogy: first, you go in with high hopes, not knowing what to expect or what will happen. Your wild expectations are soon dashed, and then you're forced to figure out what's next. You cry a lot and are embarrassed when everyone watches you spin out emotionally over this setback. Eventually, against the odds, you find love, of course.

This is the end of the story, the time when you know in your heart that it wasn't all for naught, and it is all going to be perfectly fine in the end, because these are some light biscuits you'd never know were gluten-free. They don't fall apart, and they taste pretty great with honey. True love really can happen, y'all, even in an unpredictable and stressful situation, as the result of this recipe will prove.

Makes 6; serves 2.

- 1 TABLESPOON BAKING POWDER
- 1 CUP ALMOND FLOUR
- 1/4 TEASPOON KOSHER SALT
- 2 TABLESPOONS COLD, UNSALTED BUTTER (GRATED)
- 1 LARGE EGG (BEATEN)
- 1/4 CUP 2% GREEK YOGURT

Preheat your oven to 425 degrees. Mix the baking powder, almond flour, and salt in a large bowl. Add in the cold butter; use your fingers to work the butter into the flour until there are no large clumps of butter. In a small bowl, combine the egg and yogurt. Make a well in the center of the flour mixture. Add the egg mixture. Using a rubber spatula, fold the mixture into the dry ingredients but use as few strokes as possible.

Using a medium ice cream scoop, scoop up a 1/4-cup portion of dough and place it onto a parchment-lined baking sheet. Repeat until all dough has been used. (You should get about a half-dozen biscuits from this recipe.) Be sure to leave an inch or so between each biscuit, but don't be too particular about their shape—drop biscuits are supposed to be rustic. Bake for 10 to 15 minutes or until the craggy edges are brown and crispy.

CROISSANT EGG CASSEROLE FOR TWO

You can do this! Yes, we're talking to you, especially if you've been unfairly labeled as 'the one who doesn't cook' at your house. You've got this. And your sweetie is going to be *so* surprised! Here's what to cook on Valentine's Day or any regular old day for an impressive breakfast in bed.

This casserole's kind of reminiscent of a *croque monsieur* but with our own spin, which includes goat milk brie, marinated artichoke hearts, and roasted red peppers. On the side, add some asparagus "fries" with a simple aioli for dipping. All of this is really easy to put together ahead of time, and the cool thing is that all you have to do in the morning is place the prepared casserole and asparagus in the oven. They'll be ready at the same time, and you'll look like a hero. (And if you make coffee for the both of you while you wait for it all to cook, seriously, then you're *golden*.)

Serves 2.

- 5 MINI CROISSANTS OR 3 MEDIUM (SPLIT LENGTHWISE)
- 3 LARGE EGGS
- 1/4 CUP WHIPPING CREAM
- 1 TABLESPOON KOSHER SALT
- 1 TABLESPOON CRACKED BLACK PEPPER
- 1 TABLESPOON DRIED THYME
- 1 6.5-OUNCE JAR MARINATED ARTICHOKES
- 1 11.9-OUNCE JAR ROASTED RED PEPPERS
- 1 4.4-OUNCE WHEEL OF GOAT MILK BRIE (SLICED)
- 1 TABLESPOON DIJON MUSTARD
- ASPARAGUS "FRIES" WITH SIMPLE AIOLI (RECIPE FOLLOWS)

Place the bottom portion of the croissants in a 9 x 6-inch pan and set aside the top portion of them for now. In a medium bowl, whisk together the eggs, cream, salt, pepper, and thyme. Pour the egg mixture over the bottom portions of the croissants. Place the pan in the refrigerator overnight or for at least 20 minutes. Spread the Dijon mustard evenly over the inside of the reserved top portions of the croissants and place into the fridge separately.

Once you're ready to serve, preheat your oven to 350 degrees. Drain the artichokes and peppers. Top each bottom portion of each croissant with an artichoke heart and a roasted red pepper. Top each with sliced brie. Place the pan in the oven for 20 minutes. Top with the mustard-spreaded tops and cook for another 3 to 5 minutes. Remove from the oven and serve alongside Asparagus "Fries" with Simple Aioli.

ASPARAGUS "FRIES" WITH SIMPLE AIOLI

- 1 POUND ASPARAGUS
  (BOTTOM 1/3 TRIMMED OFF)
- 1 1/2 LEMONS (DIVIDED)
- 1 TABLESPOON OLIVE OIL
- 1/4 TEASPOON KOSHER SALT
- 1/4 TEASPOON CRACKED BLACK PEPPER
- 1/4 CUP MAYONNAISE
- 1 CLOVE GARLIC (FINELY CHOPPED)
- JUICE OF 1/2 A LEMON

Preheat your oven to 350 degrees. In a large bowl, toss together the asparagus, juice from 1 lemon, olive oil, salt, and pepper. Place onto a parchment-lined baking sheet. Allow to cook for 20 to 25 minutes or until the tips are slightly browned.

In a small bowl, mix together the mayonnaise, garlic, and lemon juice to make a flavorful aioli. Serve roasted asparagus alongside small bowls of aioli and the croissant casserole.

NOTE: This recipe makes about 2 dozen sausage patties. Freeze uncooked patties in a single layer and then store them in a container or a food storage bag in the freezer for up to 3 months.

VEGAN BREAKFAST SAUSAGE

This is a vegan version of our Vegetarian Breakfast Sausage. Many TCV readers love it and depend on it, and while we sure are blushing and aw-shucks-ing about that recipe's popularity, we're still never satisfied. Simplifying and veganizing our original recipe also improved the texture and flavor. Who knew that could be done?

These are great served alongside some eggs or a tofu scrambler, or use them to make a stellar vegetarian sausage and biscuit breakfast sandwich using our Amazing Almond Flour Biscuits (page 25). You could also get creative and crumble the cooked sausage into the filling for stuffed bell peppers or crumble a little on a pizza with peppers and onions. Basically, you can use it anywhere you'd usually find regular sausage.

Makes 2 dozen sausage patties.

- 1 TEASPOON OLIVE OIL (PLUS MORE FOR PAN-FRYING)
- 1/4 CUP FINELY DICED SHALLOT
- 3 CLOVES GARLIC (FINELY DICED)
- 8 OUNCES CRIMINI MUSHROOMS (FINELY DICED)
- 1 CUP FINELY DICED CELERY (ABOUT 2 RIBS)
- 1/2 CUP FINELY DICED CARROT (1 MEDIUM)
- 1 1/2 TEASPOONS RUBBED SAGE
- 1/2 TEASPOON RED PEPPER FLAKES
- 1/4 TEASPOON CLOVE
- 1/4 TEASPOON NUTMEG
- 1 TABLESPOON SOY SAUCE (LIKE BRAGG® LIQUID AMINOS)
- 1 TABLESPOON MAPLE SYRUP
- 1 1/2 CUPS UNCOOKED QUICK-COOKING OATS
- KOSHER SALT AND CRACKED BLACK PEPPER (TO TASTE)

Heat the olive oil in a large frying pan over medium-high heat. Add the shallot, garlic, mushrooms, celery, and carrot to the pan. Stir consistently and sauté until all of the liquid has released and then evaporated; this should take about 5 minutes. Add the sage, red pepper flakes, clove, nutmeg, soy sauce, and maple syrup to the pan. Stir to incorporate and remove from heat. Allow mixture to cool. Add the uncooked quick-cooking oats and knead the mixture until everything is well-incorporated. Add salt and pepper to taste. Cover and set aside in the fridge for at least 15 minutes to allow the moisture to distribute.

Next, pinch about 2 tablespoons of the mixture off, roll it into a ball, and flatten it to make a patty. Repeat. In a medium pan over medium heat, pan-fry the patties in enough olive oil to coat the bottom of the pan until nicely browned. Drain on paper towels. Serve hot.

NOTE: All chopping can be done in the food processor to save time.

BUTTERMILK OATMEAL WITH BUTTER-POACHED PEACHES AND SORGHUM

We love oatmeal — really! It's the basis for many of our dishes, both savory and sweet. Needless to say, we think it's great, but not everyone feels that way about the humble oat. We can totally understand that, especially if all you've ever experienced of it is a dull bowl of mush for a melancholy/nutritious breakfast.

Oats, just like grits or quinoa, need a little something to wake up their flavor. That's usually something acidic like lemon juice or vinegar. Here, we used the gentle acidity of buttermilk to perk up this breakfast dish. We topped the whole thing off with a few butter-poached peaches.

Serves 2.

- 2 CUPS BUTTERMILK
- 1 CUP ROLLED OATS
- 1 HEAPING TABLESPOON LIGHT BROWN SUGAR
- 1/8 TEASPOON KOSHER SALT
- 4 RIPE PEACHES (PITTED, PEELED)
- 1 TABLESPOON UNSALTED BUTTER
- 1 TABLESPOON SORGHUM (OR MAPLE SYRUP)

In a medium pot over medium heat, warm the buttermilk and stir in the oats. Add the brown sugar and salt and stir. Cover, reduce heat to low, and continue to cook for 10 minutes; stir occasionally to prevent sticking.

Next, cut the peaches into bite-sized wedges. In a medium frying pan over medium-high heat, melt the butter, and just as it starts to brown, add the peaches. Allow them to cook for 3 minutes to lightly color on one side before turning them. Cook another 3 minutes and remove from heat. Divide the oatmeal and peaches between 2 bowls and garnish with sorghum or maple syrup.

NOTE: How to poach an egg: Fill a 10-inch frying pan half full of water and set it over medium heat. Add to it 1/4 cup white vinegar and 1/8 cup Kosher salt. That seems like a lot of salt, but think of it like salting pasta water. Once the water starts to gently simmer, slowly crack an egg into the water; open the egg halfway, let the albumen touch the water for a few seconds, and then gently allow the rest of the egg to fall into the water. This will make for a more compact egg. Remember, be patient! Once the white has mostly set, you may flip the egg using a spatula. Push the egg against the curved edge of the pan, and it should flip. Flipping it makes it cook faster, but you will lose that beautiful yellow yolk showing.

It takes about 5 minutes for a runny yolk, 6 for a slightly set yolk, and 7 to 8 to form a little, yellow, rubber ball of a yolk. You can poach the eggs ahead of time and cool them in an ice bath once they are cooked to your liking. To reheat them, place them in hot water for a few seconds.

VEGETARIAN EGG MUFFIN

These days, we're making a version of America's favorite breakfast sandwich, but with a few key changes. We like to use a whole-wheat English muffin, a perfectly poached egg, cheddar cheese, and a simple cured slice of portobello mushroom, a terrific vegetarian stand-in for Canadian bacon.

Makes 4 breakfast sandwiches.

- 2 THICK, LARGE PORTOBELLO MUSHROOMS
- 1/4 TEASPOON KOSHER SALT
- 1/2 TEASPOON SUGAR
- 4 DROPS LIQUID SMOKE

- 4 SLICES SHARP CHEDDAR CHEESE
- 4 WHOLE-WHEAT ENGLISH MUFFINS (SPLIT, TOASTED)

- 4 POACHED EGGS (SEE NOTE ON PAGE 32)
- KOSHER SALT AND CRACKED BLACK PEPPER (TO TASTE)

The first step to making this breakfast sandwich is to cure the mushroom slices overnight, so it's best to start ahead of time. Slice the mushrooms about 1/4-inch thick starting at the top of the mushroom and working across parallel to the gills. (You should be able to get 3 to 4 slices out of each mushroom before getting to the gills.) Save the gills and the rest of the scraps for another use. Mix the salt and sugar together in a small bowl. Into a glass container, place a slice of the mushroom and sprinkle it with the salt and sugar mixture. Continue until all slices and seasoning have been used. Add the liquid smoke, cover, and place in the fridge overnight. The salt and sugar will draw a lot of moisture from the mushrooms.

To assemble, place the cheese on the toasted muffin. Sear the cured mushroom slices in a a hot, dry pan for a few seconds until brown. Place 1 or 2 mushroom slices on top of the cheese, top with a poached egg, salt, pepper, and the muffin top. Wrap it up and take it on-the-go or sit down and enjoy it with a cup of espresso.

TOMATO MATZO BREI AND TRUFFLED LATKES

Our version of matzo brei uses both soaked matzo and crumbled matzo to offer two distinct textures of the same ingredient. We also add chopped tomatoes to give it a little something extra. We served the Tomato Matzo Brei on top of simple-but-delicious Truffled Latkes. Make these ahead of time and warm them in the oven. The edges are crisp, and the center is nice and creamy.

Serves 4.

- 1/2 CUP WHOLE MILK
- 2 MATZO CRACKERS (CRUMBLED, DIVIDED)
- 3/4 CUP TOMATOES
- KOSHER SALT AND CRACKED BLACK PEPPER (TO TASTE)
- 1 TABLESPOON UNSALTED BUTTER
- 5 LARGE EGGS (BEATEN)
- TRUFFLED LATKES (RECIPE FOLLOWS)
- 1/4 CUP SOUR CREAM
- CHOPPED CHIVES (TO GARNISH)

In a medium bowl, add the milk and one of the crumbled matzo crackers. Add the tomatoes to the bowl as well. Season with salt and pepper to taste. In a large pan over medium-low heat, melt the butter and then add the eggs and the soaked matzo mixture. Stir continually until the eggs are just set. Add the remaining crumbled matzo cracker and stir to incorporate. Place Matzo Brei egg mixture into a bowl until ready to serve.

To serve, spoon about 1/4 cup of Matzo Brei on top of each Truffled Latke followed by a teaspoon of sour cream, a sprinkling of chopped chives, and salt and pepper to taste.

TRUFFLED LATKES

- 3 CUPS SHREDDED IDAHO POTATO (ABOUT 1 LARGE)
- 1/2 TEASPOON TRUFFLE SALT
- 1 LARGE EGG (BEATEN)
- 1/4 CUP ALL-PURPOSE FLOUR
- 1/4 CUP CHOPPED CHIVES
- CRACKED BLACK PEPPER (TO TASTE)
- 1 TABLESPOON OLIVE OIL

In a large bowl, mix the potato, truffle salt, egg, flour, chives, and pepper until well incorporated. In a large pan over medium heat, bring the oil up to temperature. Add 1/4-cup mounds of the potato mixture to the oil. This will need to be done in batches. Cook for 5 minutes per side or until browned. Keep warm in a low oven until ready to serve.

FRENCH BREAKFAST RADISH WITH BAGUETTE AND HONEY

In our first cookbook, Chef John Currence closed his foreword by saying, "Radishes with softened butter are WAY underappreciated." Technically, that qualifies as the first recipe in *The Southern Vegetarian: 100 Down-Home Recipes for the Modern Table*. We hear you loud and clear, Chef! We agree that simplicity can be beautiful, and we think about your quote every time we try this beautiful combo.

Here we've switched out softened butter for a buttery soft brie and paired the whole thing with local honey to balance out the bite of the spicy radishes. Now just imagine yourself in a chateau on the French countryside on a beautiful morning. Have some French press coffee and a leisurely breakfast.

Serves 2.

- 1/2 LARGE BAGUETTE (SLICED INTO 12 ROUNDS)
- 6 MEDIUM FRENCH BREAKFAST RADISHES (SLICED)
- 1 7-OUNCE WHEEL OR WEDGE OF DOUBLE-CREAM BRIE
- 2 TABLESPOONS HONEY
- 1 TEASPOON KOSHER SALT
- 1 TEASPOON CRACKED BLACK PEPPER

In a cast-iron grill pan over medium heat, grill the baguette slices on one side for 3 minutes or until well-marked by the grill grates. Set aside. Arrange the radishes, baguette, and brie on a cutting board or large plate. Mix the the salt and pepper in a small bowl. To eat, arrange a slice of brie and a few slices of radish on a piece of baguette. Drizzle the top with honey.

APPETIZERS & SNACKS

. . . .

YOUNG COCONUT CEVICHE

Making this dish throughout the year calls up memories of warm summer days. It's a great dish for any season, and it's so easy you won't believe it. The rich coconut meat, crunchy veggies, and bright acidity from the lime juice makes for one tasty ceviche. You don't even have to turn on the oven. Just crack open a coconut, chop few things, and you have a snack in a flash made from real food.

Serves 6.

- 1 FRESH YOUNG COCONUT
- JUICE OF 2 MEDIUM LIMES
- 1/2 CUP DICED ROMA TOMATO
- 1/2 CUP SEEDED AND DICED ENGLISH CUCUMBER
- 1/2 CUP DICED RED ONION

- 1 SERRANO PEPPER (SEEDED AND FINELY DICED)
- 1/4 CUP CHOPPED CILANTRO
- DASH OF HOT SAUCE
- KOSHER SALT AND CRACKED BLACK PEPPER (TO TASTE)

- TORTILLA CHIPS (OR 4 CRISPY TOSTADAS)
- MAYONNAISE (OPTIONAL)
- SLICED RADISHES AND AVOCADO (TO GARNISH)

Using a large spoon, gently scrape the coconut meat out of the coconut. (Make sure to scrape off any bits of shell that may be attached.) Cut coconut meat into small chunks and place in a container with the lime juice. Allow coconut to rest in the fridge for about 30 minutes in order for it to marinate.

In a medium bowl, toss together the coconut and lime juice mixture, tomato, cucumber, onion, serrano pepper, cilantro, hot sauce, and salt and pepper to taste. Serve like a dip with chips for an appetizer or on crispy tostadas slathered in mayo, topped with ceviche, and garnished with radish and avocado for a great meal.

NOTE: To crack open the coconut, set it on a steady cutting board, take a cleaver or large knife in your dominant hand, and put your other hand firmly behind your back. DO NOT EVER STEADY OR HOLD THE COCONUT WITH YOUR OTHER HAND! Take aim and chop the cleaver into the top of the coconut with enough force to break through the tough skin. Keeping one hand still behind your back, repeat this four times taking careful aim each time so that you make a square-shaped opening. Using the tip of your cleaver, pry the cut part away to reveal an opening in the top of the coconut. It will be full of delicious coconut water. Pour the coconut water through a strainer and into a glass. Enjoy the coconut water while you continue to prepare the recipe. Gently scape the coconut meat out with a spoon and set aside for the ceviche.

FIGS IN A BLANKET

This dish was inspired by a late-night snack at Fat Possum Hollow last summer. I'd been asked to stay a few days and photograph the place, and I'd brought along walnuts and also some figs I'd picked that morning from one of our trees for a quick snack. The cabin I was staying in had one thing in the fridge: American cheese singles. Famished after a day of shooting photos, I wrapped my figs and walnuts in the cheese slices and let out a little laugh as I thought to myself, "I am now eating figs in a blanket."

When you get ready to try this one, look for figs that are just getting ripe and avoid ones that are already soft—they won't fare so well in the oven. What you'll end up with is a snack that's on the savory side of sweet due to the smoked cheddar and cracked black pepper, and they're just rich enough. They're so simple to prepare and, as a bonus, will probably elicit a bemused laugh or two from, you know, the usual pigs-in-a-blanket enthusiasts.

Makes 16 Figs in a Blanket.

- 8 EXTRA-LARGE FRESH FIGS
- 1 TEASPOON OLIVE OIL
- 1 TEASPOON SHERRY VINEGAR
- KOSHER SALT AND CRACKED BLACK PEPPER (TO TASTE)
- 1 TUBE OF CRESCENT ROLLS
- 3 OUNCES SMOKED CHEDDAR CHEESE (CUT INTO 16 SQUARES)
- 16 WALNUT HALVES

Preheat your oven to 350 degrees. Cut the figs in half and drizzle them with oil and vinegar. Add salt and pepper to taste.

Using a pizza cutter, slice each pre-cut triangle of dough in half to create 16 long, skinny triangles. Stack one fig half, one square of cheese, and one walnut half on each triangle. Starting at the fat end of the dough triangle, roll up the fig, cheese, and walnut stack. Place the resulting roll cheese-side-up on a parchment-lined baking sheet. Repeat until all figs are used.

Bake for 12 to 14 minutes or until rolls are golden brown. Be sure to allow them to cool for 10 minutes.

BAKED CAULIFLOWER WINGS WITH BLACK AND BLEU DRESSING

Wings: we love 'em. Problem is, they're usually chicken. Coming up with a suitable non-processed substitute was tough, to say the least. So when we tried cauliflower, we found that it soaked up the flavors nicely, and it had plenty of texture. This would be a great and sort of amusing thing to set out on the table on game day. Everyone will love this app because it's spicy and rich, but far less so than its fried, feathered cousin.

Serves 4 as an appetizer.

- BLACK AND BLEU DRESSING (RECIPE FOLLOWS)
- 1 HEAD OF CAULIFLOWER (BROKEN INTO LARGE FLORETS)
- 2 TABLESPOONS OLIVE OIL
- 1 TABLESPOON RANCH DIP MIX
- 3/4 CUP HOT WING SAUCE
- 2 CARROTS (PEELED AND CUT INTO MATCHSTICKS)
- 2 RIBS CELERY (PEELED AND CUT INTO MATCHSTICKS)

Preheat your oven to 425 degrees. Make the dressing first.

In a large bowl, toss the cauliflower with the olive oil and the Ranch dip mix. Place in a single layer onto a large parchment-lined baking sheet. Roast in the oven for 20 minutes.

Toss the roasted cauliflower in the wing sauce mixture. Return the cauliflower to the parchment-lined baking sheet and cook for another 15 minutes.

Serve with the Black and Bleu dressing, carrots, and celery.

BLACK AND BLEU DRESSING

- 1/2 CUP CRUMBLED BLEU CHEESE
- 1/2 CUP GREEK YOGURT
- 1 TABLESPOON SHERRY VINEGAR
- 1 TEASPOON CRACKED BLACK PEPPER (TO TASTE)
- 1/4 TEASPOON KOSHER SALT (TO TASTE)

In a medium bowl, whisk together the bleu cheese, yogurt, vinegar, pepper, and salt. Add salt to taste and set aside in the fridge. (Makes about 1 cup.)

PASTRAMI-CURED BEETS

This dish is as easy as it is delicious; requiring only a few minutes of hands-on time, it easily can be made ahead. Serve it on a charcuterie plate before dinner with some spicy mustard and pickles or on a sandwich for a great picnic option.

Serves 4.

- 1 TABLESPOON CRACKED BLACK PEPPER
- 1 TEASPOON GROUND CORIANDER
- 1 TEASPOON SMOKED PAPRIKA
- 1 TEASPOON KOSHER SALT
- 1/2 TEASPOON GRANULATED GARLIC
- 1 TABLESPOON OLIVE OIL
- 3 LARGE BEETS (PEELED)

Make the pastrami cure in a medium bowl by mixing the pepper, coriander, paprika, salt, and garlic together. Drizzle the olive oil over the beets so that they're evenly covered; this will allow the cure to stick to them. Liberally coat each beet with the cure on both sides and place in a covered container in the fridge for at least 1 hour or up to 24 hours.

Preheat your oven to 350 degrees. Wrap each beet in foil and place into a casserole dish. Bake for 1 1/2 hours or until tender. Allow beets to cool completely. Slice thinly using a knife or a mandoline.

CARROT "LOX" WITH RED ONION, CAPERS, DILL, AND CRÉME FRAÎCHE

At parties, we always eye the requisite beautiful dish of smoked salmon with all of the garnishes; we love the color of the red onion against the green capers and the bright color of the fish itself. So of course we were inspired to create a vegetable version!

Here, the thin slices of carrot get the same sort of cure one might use on salmon. It's simply a mix of salt, pepper, and brown sugar. We used smoked salt in order to skip the extra step of smoking the dish on the smoker, and the result's great. In fact, these may the the best carrots you've ever had. So set this out at your next gathering or party. It makes a delicious conversation piece.

Serves 6 to 8.

- 1 POUND ORGANIC CARROTS (ABOUT 5 TO 6 LARGE)
- 2 TEASPOONS SMOKED SEA SALT
- 2 TEASPOONS LIGHT BROWN SUGAR
- 2 TEASPOONS CRACKED BLACK PEPPER
- 2 LARGE EGGS (BEATEN)
- ZEST OF 1 LEMON
- 1 TABLESPOON OLIVE OIL
- DICED RED ONION, CAPERS (IN SALT OR BRINE), FRESH DILL, CRÉME FRAÎCHE, LEMON WEDGES (TO GARNISH)

Peel and very thinly slice the carrots longways on a mandoline. In a small bowl, combine the smoked salt, light brown sugar, and black pepper. Layer the carrot slices in a large bowl and add a pinch of the spice mixture to each layer until all of the carrot slices and spice mixture are used. Set this aside for 30 minutes. The salt will soften the carrots and leach out much of their liquid.

Remove the carrots from the bowl and discard the liquid and spices that have gathered at the bottom. Add the carrots, eggs, and lemon zest back to the bowl and toss to coat each strand with egg. Line a 1/4-sheet pan with parchment paper and brush it with olive oil. Preheat your oven to 350 degrees. Starting with a long strand of carrot, lay it flat across the parchment paper. Continue to lay the carrots one after the other overlapping them almost completely. Pair shorter strands together to span the length of the dish. Once all the carrots are laid out, brush the top with the egg that remains in the bottom of the bowl. Cover the dish tightly with aluminum foil to seal in the moisture. Bake for 30 to 35 minutes or until carrots are just tender. Keep covered and allow to cool completely.

Uncover and slice it down the middle using a sharp knife. Serve at room temperature garnished with red onion, capers, and fresh dill. Add créme fraîche and lemon wedges on the side.

NOTE: Once you've diced the onion, place it in a bowl of cold water for a few minutes and then drain it. This will wash away any of the astringent taste associated with raw onion. It's a good idea to do the same to the capers.

PUPUSAS WITH PICKLED LOROCO FLOWER

David, the talented and methodical guy who did the brick work on our backyard pizza oven, hails from El Salvador. During the hours it took us to lay out and build that oven, we got to know each other by talking about all sorts of things. I had lots of questions for him about Salvadoran food. I asked him, "So, it's a typical weekday, not a special occasion, and if you're going to eat a home-cooked meal for dinner, what are you making?" "Pupusas with loroco flowers!" he told me. Honestly, I didn't know what either of those things were, so he patiently explained it all to me.

He said that pupusas are like rustic, thick tortillas stuffed with all manner of things, and loroco flowers are flower buds served fresh or pickled—a regional delicacy in El Salvador. So that week, Amy and I set out to find loroco flowers, and lo and behold, they had them at the local supermarket for about $3. We bought them, took them home, and cracked open the giant jar. It's always exciting to try a new food for the first time. They are briny from the pickling, lightly bitter, and have the texture of snow peas...we like them! You should give them a try, too.

Makes 4 pupusas; serves 2.

- 1 CUP MASA (FOR TORTILLAS)
- 1/4 CUP NON-HYDROGENATED VEGETABLE SHORTENING
- 1/2 CUP VEGETABLE BROTH
- 1/2 CUP PICKLED LOROCO FLOWERS

- 1 CUP SHREDDED CHIHUAHUA CHEESE (OR MOZZARELLA)
- 1/4 TEASPOON GRANULATED GARLIC
- 1/4 TEASPOON CUMIN
- 1/4 TEASPOON ANCHO CHILI POWDER

- 1/2 TEASPOON HOT SAUCE (MORE TO GARNISH)
- OLIVE OIL FOR PAN-FRYING
- LIMES, CILANTRO, AVOCADO, PURPLE CABBAGE SLAW (PAGE 88), AND SALSA (TO GARNISH)

In a medium bowl, add the masa, shortening, and broth and then mix it all together to form a slightly stiff yet pliable dough. Add a teaspoon or two of water or broth if the mixture is too dry. Cover and let stand for 10 minutes. In a separate medium bowl, add the loroco flowers, cheese, garlic, cumin, chili, and hot sauce and then toss so that all ingredients are well-incorporated.

Divide the dough into eight equal segments and roll each into a ball. Place one of the dough balls into the palm of your hand, smash it flat with your other palm, add 1/4 of the cheese mixture to the center, add a second flattened dough ball on top of that, and work it into a patty about the size of a typical hamburger while pinching the sides together to seal. Repeat.

In a large pan over medium heat, add enough oil to just coat the bottom of the pan. Pan-fry each patty for 4 to 5 minutes per side or until nicely colored. Serve hot and garnish however you please; options are listed in the ingredients list.

BAGNA CAUDA SMASHED CHICKPEA DIP

At the start of any get-together, we typically set out a bunch of cheese, bread, nuts, and olives so everyone has something to munch on while hanging out in the kitchen as we cook. But the first time we used our wood-fired oven to cook pizzas, we wondered what we should serve as an appetizer if cheese was going to be melted all over the main dish. Pizza's a tough dinner to round out—you don't want the appetizer or the dessert to be too similar to it.

So we grilled up some thin slices of eggplant and zucchini and roasted a few red peppers like they do at one of our favorite places, Bari Ristorante in Memphis. To stand in for the cheese, we made smashed chickpeas flavored with minced garlic, rosemary, and capers, much like the classic Italian bagna cauda, but with capers subbed in for the anchovies.

Serves 4 to 6.

- 3 CLOVES GARLIC
- 1 TEASPOON CAPERS
- 2 TABLESPOONS OLIVE OIL (DIVIDED)
- 1 2-INCH SPRING OF FRESH ROSEMARY (STEM REMOVED, MINCED)
- 1/3 CUP WHITE WINE (LIKE PINOT GRIGIO)
- 1/2 TEASPOON CHAMPAGNE VINEGAR
- 1/8 TEASPOON RED PEPPER FLAKES
- KOSHER SALT AND CRACKED BLACK PEPPER (TO TASTE)
- 1 CAN CHICKPEAS (RINSED AND DRAINED)

Mince the garlic and the capers together. In a medium skillet over medium heat, heat 1 1/2 tablespoons of the olive oil and add the minced garlic and the capers. Cook until fragrant, but don't let the garlic burn. Add the rosemary and then add the wine and vinegar. Add the red pepper, salt, and pepper. Cook until wine is reduced by half. Add the chickpeas and smash using a potato masher. If it's too thick, add water to thin it slightly so that it's spreadable. Place into a serving bowl and garnish with the remaining olive oil. Serve alongside grilled vegetables, sliced ciabatta, and olives.

ROMESCO CROSTINI WITH CHARRED SPRING ONIONS

Romesco is a traditional sauce made with almonds and peppers, and it has innumerable preparations in Spain. In the springtime, charred onions are dipped into Romesco for a special treat. This playful take on that tradition is the perfect thing to set out at a party along with some olives and Marcona almonds.

Everyone will really love onions cooked this way. The burnt exterior is pulled away to reveal a soft and almost candy-like interior that's a great foil for the spicy Romesco spread.

Serves 4.

- 12 TO 15 PURPLE OR GREEN SPRING ONIONS
- 1 MEDIUM HEAD GARLIC
- 1 MEDIUM RED PEPPER
- 1/3 CUP ROASTED AND SALTED ALMONDS
- 1/3 CUP CHOPPED SUN-DRIED TOMATOES (SOFTENED IN WARM WATER)

- 1/3 CUP TORN BAGUETTE
- 1 TEASPOON RED PEPPER FLAKES
- 1 TABLESPOON OLIVE OIL
- 1 TEASPOON SHERRY VINEGAR
- 1/2 TEASPOON SMOKED PAPRIKA

- 12 TO 15 GRILLED OR TOASTED THIN BAGUETTE SLICES (FOR SERVING)
- 12 TO 15 SLICES OF MANCHEGO CHEESE (FOR SERVING)

Preheat your outdoor grill to high heat. Place the green onion, garlic, and red pepper on the grill and turn frequently until completely charred on all sides; the amount of time on the grill will vary depending on how hot your grill gets. Place it all into a bowl and cover with foil until it's cool enough to handle. Cut the top off of the bulb of garlic. Peel and seed the roasted red pepper.

Into the work bowl of your food processor, squeeze the soft garlic from the head, add the roasted red pepper, almonds, sun-dried tomatoes, bread, red pepper flakes, olive oil, sherry vinegar, and smoked paprika. Run the food processor until a paste forms—you're looking for a thick and spreadable consistency.

To serve, slather about a teaspoon of Romesco sauce onto a toasted baguette. Top that with a peeled charred onion. Simply squeeze the onion bulb from the root end to reveal a sweet, translucent morsel. Top with a slice of Manchego cheese.

PEPPER JELLY RANGOONS

In the South, we love our pepper jelly—especially in the wintertime when the abundance of hot peppers from the garden is just a distant memory. This dish always takes us back to summer days of high humidity, fresh air, and gorgeous sunshine. The sweet-hot jelly is tempered by the cream cheese. (Hey, don't get too anxious to eat these right away; let them cool or you'll surely burn your little mouth!)

Makes 12 rangoons.

- 12 WONTON WRAPPERS
- 6 TO 8 TEASPOONS CREAM CHEESE
- 6 TO 8 TEASPOONS SAMBAL PEPPER JELLY (RECIPE FOLLOWS)
- 1 TABLESPOON OLIVE OIL
- KOSHER SALT AND CRACKED BLACK PEPPER (TO TASTE)
- CHOPPED CHIVES (TO GARNISH)

Preheat your oven to 350 degrees. On a large, rimmed, parchment-lined baking sheet, lay out the 12 wonton wrappers. Into the center of each, place about 1/2 teaspoon each of cream cheese and 1/2 teaspoon of pepper jelly. Have a small bowl of water at the ready. Dip your finger in the water and run it along 2 sides of the wonton wrapper. Fold wonton into a triangle and press the edges together to seal. Repeat.

Brush the tops of the folded wontons with olive oil and sprinkle with salt and pepper. Bake for 10 minutes and then flip each rangoon using kitchen tongs. Bake them for another 10 minutes or until brown and crispy. Allow them to cool for at least 5 minutes. Garnish with chopped chives and serve.

SAMBAL PEPPER JELLY

- 1 TABLESPOON HONEY
- 1 TABLESPOON SAMBAL

In a small bowl, mix honey and sambal together until combined. (Makes about 1/8 cup.)

BETTER JALAPEÑO POPPERS

Our version of the omnipresent bar snack is 'better' because it's crunchier, more delicious, and un-fried, unlike its greasy predecessors. So what are you waiting for? Watch a sports game and eat these jalapeño poppers like a sophisticated person...with a fork.

Makes 8 to 12 poppers.

- 4 LARGE OR 6 MEDIUM JALAPEÑO PEPPERS (HALVED LENGTHWISE, SEEDS REMOVED)
- 2 OUNCES NEUFCHÂTEL CHEESE
- 1 CUP SHREDDED CHEDDAR

- 1/4 TEASPOON GRANULATED GARLIC
- 1/4 TEASPOON CUMIN
- 1/4 TEASPOON CHIPOTLE PEPPER POWDER
- ZEST OF 1/2 LIME
- 1 LARGE EGG (BEATEN)

- 3/4 CUP PANKO BREAD CRUMBS
- 1 TEASPOON OLIVE OIL
- SOUR CREAM AND FRESH CHIVES (TO GARNISH)

Place the seeded, cut peppers cut-side-up on a parchment-lined baking sheet. Preheat your oven to 350 degrees. In a medium bowl, mix the Neufchâtel, cheddar, garlic, cumin, chipotle, and lime zest together until well-incorporated. Divide the mixture among the peppers by stuffing them until the mixture is even with the sides of the pepper.

In a medium bowl, mix the egg with the panko until well-incorporated. Place the mixture atop the cheese-stuffed peppers until all of the panko is used. Drizzle peppers with olive oil. Bake for 20 minutes or until golden brown. Garnish with sour cream and chives and serve immediately.

CHIPOTLE SOUR CREAM

- 1 CUP MEXICAN CREMA OR SOUR CREAM
- 2 CHIPOTLE PEPPERS (FROM A CAN)
- 1 CLOVE GARLIC

Place crema or sour cream, chipotle, and garlic in a food processor and blend until smooth. Set aside in the fridge until ready to use. (Makes about 1 cup.)

HUITLACOCHE AND SWEET POTATO QUESADILLAS WITH CHIPOTLE CREAM

Huitlacoche, also known as the Mexican truffle (or by its much less appealing common name, corn smut), is a mushroom-like fungus that grows on corn. It invades the plant through the stalk and feeds off of the kernels. When you peel back the corn silk of a plant that has been infected with the huitlacoche fungus, it looks like the corn has gone horribly wrong. It's kind of chunky and looks like a smear of black ink. That aside, it's delicious. We'd describe the taste as earthy, bittersweet, with a faint herbal flavor of oregano. It's quite a delicacy in Mexico. It hasn't quite caught on here in the states.

You can find huitlacoche in some Mexican supermarkets if you look, but Amazon also has a few vendors that supply it. These quesadillas are a great thing to make when you're ready to put your corn smut to good use. The mild sweetness of the sweet potato plays nicely off of the bittersweetness of the huitlacoche, and the creamy/spicy blend of the chipotle sour cream is the perfect garnish.

Serves 2.

- 1 TABLESPOON OLIVE OIL (PLUS MORE FOR COOKING THE QUESADILLAS)
- 1 1/4 CUPS FINELY DICED SWEET POTATO (1 SMALL)
- KOSHER SALT AND CRACKED BLACK PEPPER (TO TASTE)
- 7 OUNCES OAXACA OR MOZZARELLA CHEESE (SHREDDED)
- 7 SMALL CORN OR FLOUR TORTILLAS
- 7-OUNCE CAN OF HUITLACOCHE
- CHIPOTLE SOUR CREAM (RECIPE ON PREVIOUS PAGE)
- CHIVES (TO GARNISH)

In a medium pan over medium heat, heat the olive oil until it shimmers. Add the sweet potato and cook, turning often, until it has softened. Add salt and pepper to taste. Set aside. Assemble the quesadillas by layering in equal amounts of cheese onto each tortilla and then continuing with equal amounts of huitlacoche and sweet potato. Close each tortilla. In a medium pan over medium heat, add a touch of oil and cook each quesadilla until it's lightly brown and the cheese has melted (about 2 minutes per side). Garnish with chipotle sour cream and chives.

KIMCHI AND PEANUT DUMPLINGS

The great thing about these dumplings it is that they're really simple and basically only require three ingredients. We use the kimchi we make from our own recipe (page 256), but a good-quality store-bought jar of it is fine here, especially if you're in a rush to make a great appetizer for a dinner party or just want to make yourself one super-stellar snack.

Makes about 2 dozen dumplings.

- 1 12-OUNCE PACKAGE OF WONTON WRAPPERS
- 2 CUPS KIMCHI (DRAINED, FINELY CHOPPED)

- 1/2 CUP CHOPPED ROASTED AND SALTED PEANUTS
- 2 TABLESPOONS OLIVE OIL

- CHIVES AND SESAME OIL (TO GARNISH)
- VEGETARIAN FISH SAUCE (PAGE 254) OR SOY SAUCE (FOR DIPPING)

With a small bowl of water at the ready, place one wonton in the palm of your hand. Place about 1 tablespoon of kimchi in the center, and sprinkle a few chopped peanuts on top of the kimchi. Dip your finger in the bowl of water and run it along two edges of the wonton, fold it in half so it looks like a triangle, and pinch the edges so the dumpling stays closed. Place seam-side-up on a piece of floured parchment. Repeat until all kimchi has been used. (Know that it's fine for this part to be done ahead.)

In a medium frying pan (one that has a lid) over medium-high heat, heat a tablespoon of olive oil until it shimmers. Place 8 to 10 wontons in the oil. Once the bottom of the dumplings start to brown, carefully pour in about 1/4 cup of water and place the lid onto the pan. Remove from heat. Allow the lid to stay on for 2 minutes in order to steam the dumplings. Garnish with chives and sesame oil. Serve immediately with vegetarian fish sauce or soy sauce on the side for dipping.

INDIAN NACHOS WITH MINT RAITA AND BLACK MUSTARD SEED

One summer, we made some nachos from the tomatoes, mint, okra, and peppers that we grew in our small raised bed garden. We thought why not try this classic dish with a little twist: Indian flavors! Think of it like this: a simple vegetable curry on a tiny papadum with a fragrant, creamy sauce. Load up papadum chips in a single layer onto a plate and microwave them for a minute to get these going.

Serves 2.

- 1 SHALLOT
- 2 GARLIC CLOVES
- 1 SMALL JALAPEÑO PEPPER
- 1 SMALL PIECE FRESH GINGER (PEELED)
- 1 TABLESPOON UNSALTED BUTTER
- 1/2 TEASPOON CORIANDER

- 1/2 TEASPOON CUMIN
- 1/2 TEASPOON CURRY
- 1/2 CUP COCONUT MILK
- 1 TABLESPOON OLIVE OIL
- 1 CUP SMALL DICED POTATOES
- 1/8 CUP THINLY SLICED OKRA

- 1/8 CUP SMALL DICED TOMATOES
- 1/8 CUP ENGLISH PEAS
- 2 DOZEN SMALL PAPADUMS
- MINT RAITA (RECIPE FOLLOWS)
- BLACK MUSTARD SEED

Finely chop the shallot, garlic, jalapeño, and ginger in a food processor. Melt butter in a large frying pan over medium heat and add the coriander, cumin, and curry. Once the spices become fragrant, add the chopped shallot, garlic, jalapeño, and ginger mixture. Cook for two minutes. Add the coconut milk and stir. Set sauce aside. In the same pan over medium-high heat, sauté the potatoes in the olive oil until golden and tender. This should take about 4 minutes. Add the okra, tomatoes, and peas and heat through. Add the sauce and remove from heat. Arrange papadums on a platter and top each with about a teaspoon of the vegetable curry. Garnish with mint raita and a pinch of black mustard seed.

MINT RAITA

- 1/4 CUP MINT
- 1/4 CUP YOGURT
- ZEST FROM 1 LIME
- 1/2 TEASPOON SUGAR
- 1 TABLESPOON WATER

Blend all ingredients in a food processor until mint is finely chopped. (Makes about 1/2 cup.)

PATATAS BRAVAS WITH VEGAN AVOCADO AIOLI

Our friend Kelly is always traveling, but he stopped by for tapas at our house when he'd returned from his latest jaunt, and he surprised us with the highest compliment about the meal we'd put together. "I feel like I'm back in Spain," he remarked as he surveyed one of the dishes set out on our dining room table: our take on patatas bravas with a vegan avocado aioli plus a generous hand with sriracha.

It's rich and spicy comfort food that we make our own by baking the potatoes rather than frying them and replacing the traditional aioli with blended avocado. This transforms the dish into something healthier without sacrificing flavor.

Serves 4.

- 4 CUPS PEELED AND CUBED YUKON GOLD POTATOES (ABOUT 6 MEDIUM)
- 1 TEASPOON KOSHER SALT
- 1 TEASPOON SPANISH SMOKED PAPRIKA
- 1 TABLESPOON OLIVE OIL
- 1/4 CUP SRIRACHA HOT SAUCE
- VEGAN AVOCADO AIOLI (RECIPE FOLLOWS)
- CHOPPED FLAT-LEAF PARSLEY (TO GARNISH)

In a large bowl, toss together the potatoes, salt, paprika, and olive oil. Arrange the coated potatoes in a single layer onto a large, parchment-lined baking sheet, place into a cold oven, close the oven door, and set the temperature to 450 degrees. The potatoes will be golden and crispy in 25 minutes.

While the potatoes are cooking, prepare the Vegan Avocado Aioli. Next, swirl about 1 teaspoon of Sriracha directly onto each of the four small plates.

Once the potatoes are ready, add one cup of them to each plate. Using a pair of kitchen shears, cut off and discard one corner of the sandwich bag that contains the Vegan Avocado Aioli. Squeeze the bag to garnish each plate with a swirl of Vegan Avocado Aioli and then a small sprinkle of chopped parsley. Serve each plate with toothpicks as utensils for an authentic tapas-bar feel.

VEGAN AVOCADO AIOLI

- JUICE OF 1 LEMON
- 1 MEDIUM CLOVE GARLIC
- 1 LARGE AVOCADO (PITTED, PEELED)
- 1/4 TEASPOON KOSHER SALT

Into your food processor or mini-prep, add the lemon juice, garlic, avocado flesh, and salt. Blend until very smooth. Using a rubber spatula, transfer the purée to a zip-top sandwich bag. Press out all of the air before closing; this will keep the avocado from turning brown. Place the bag in the fridge until you're ready to garnish the patatas bravas. (Makes about 1 cup.)

RAITA DIPPING SAUCE

- 3/4 CUP VERY FINELY DICED CUCUMBERS (PEELED, SEEDED)
- 1 CUP 2% GREEK YOGURT
- 1/4 TEASPOON KOSHER SALT
- 1/2 TEASPOON SUGAR

In a medium bowl, mix the cucumbers, yogurt, salt, sugar, and mint until combined. Set aside in the refrigerator until ready to serve. (Double the recipe if you plan on serving all 50 samosas at once.) (Makes about 1 3/4 cups.)

SAMOSAS WITH RAITA DIPPING SAUCE

This is a great recipe if you're looking for a dish to set out at a party. It's more creative than chips and dip—and it makes a ton! You can fry the samosas ahead of time and just warm them in the oven before you serve them.

These also freeze well, so if you make the whole batch and just eat a few, that's no problem. Just lay the un-fried samosas on a cutting board in a single layer and stick them in the freezer for a couple of hours and then transfer them to a container until you're ready to use them.

Serves 10.

- 1 TABLESPOON UNSALTED BUTTER
- 1 TABLESPOON OLIVE OIL
- 1 CUP DICED ONION
- 1 TABLESPOON MAHARAJAH CURRY POWDER (MAY SUBSTITUTE HOT OR SWEET CURRY POWDER)
- 1 TEASPOON CORIANDER
- 1 TEASPOON CUMIN
- 1/2 TEASPOON GRANULATED GARLIC

- 1/2 TEASPOON KOSHER SALT
- 4 CUPS DICED POTATO (ABOUT 3 MEDIUM, PEELED)
- 1 13.5-OUNCE CAN COCONUT MILK
- 1/4 TEASPOON GREEN CARDAMOM SEEDS (NOT THE PODS)
- 1/4 TEASPOON METHI (FENUGREEK) SEEDS (OPTIONAL)
- 1 CUP FROZEN GREEN PEAS

- 1 TEASPOON SUGAR
- 1 TEASPOON WHITE VINEGAR
- 1/4 CUP FINELY CHOPPED GOLDEN RAISINS
- SAMBAL (TO TASTE)
- 1 12-OUNCE PACKAGE WONTON WRAPPERS
- VEGETABLE OIL FOR FRYING
- RAITA DIPPING SAUCE (RECIPE ON PREVIOUS PAGE)

In a large frying pan over medium-high heat, melt the butter and add the oil. Add the onion, curry powder, coriander, cumin, garlic, and salt. Cook while stirring constantly for about 4 minutes. Add the potato, coconut milk, cardamom, and methi seeds to the mix. Cook uncovered until the potatoes are tender (about 10 minutes). Using a potato masher, mash the mixture. Add the peas, sugar, vinegar, and raisins to the mixture. Taste mixture and add enough sambal to give it a little heat; we use 1 teaspoon. Stir to incorporate. Set aside to cool.

Place 1 tablespoon of the mixture into the center of a wonton wrapper, dampen two edges with a tiny bit of water to help it seal, fold it into a triangle, and pinch the edges together to ensure a tight seal. (It's best to use a small ice cream scoop to transfer the filling, and it's very helpful to have a small bowl of water handy in order to help seal the samosas quickly.)

In a large frying pan over medium heat, heat 1/2 inch of vegetable oil. Fry samosas in batches of 5 for just about 30 seconds per side or until golden and crispy.

VEGGIE-PACKED NAPA CABBAGE WRAPS WITH SPICY PEANUT SAUCE

We were so happy to have our contractor friends step in and renovate our kitchen after a dishwasher leak stealthily did its damage one summer. As a thank-you, we made all the food at a party Walker and his wife Nikki hosted at their home. Traditionally, this holiday shindig has been all about Memphis BBQ. As we planned and prepped, we wondered how our dishes would be received by people who might not usually gravitate toward (or even want?) vegetarian food. It wasn't like we were going to serve "a bunch of tofu or something," we reassured the hosts. That might be too crazy to do for this crowd.

Well, we actually ended up doing just that when we made these cabbage wraps! Tofu has a great, meaty texture when it's cooked correctly, and it just makes sense here in an Asian-inspired dish. These wraps are packed with vegetables, and the peanut sauce that accompanies them is awesome even on its own. We think they'll win you over, too.

Serves 4.

- 1 HEAD OF NAPA CABBAGE
- 1 8-OUNCE PACKAGE CRIMINI MUSHROOMS
- 2 MEDIUM CARROTS (ROUGHLY CHOPPED)
- 1 RED BELL PEPPER
- 1-INCH PIECE FRESH GINGER

- 3 LARGE CLOVES GARLIC
- 1/2 TEASPOON CHINESE FIVE-SPICE
- 1/4 TEASPOON CRACKED BLACK PEPPER
- 1/4 TEASPOON KOSHER SALT
- 2 TABLESPOONS OLIVE OIL (DIVIDED)

- 1 8-OUNCE PACKAGE EXTRA-FIRM TOFU (DRAINED, CUBED)
- 1/2 CUP ROASTED AND SALTED PEANUTS
- 1/4 CUP CILANTRO LEAVES
- SPICY PEANUT SAUCE (RECIPE FOLLOWS)

SPICY PEANUT SAUCE

- 1/4 CUP PEANUT BUTTER
- 1 TABLESPOON TOASTED SESAME OIL
- 1 TABLESPOON BROWN RICE VINEGAR
- 1 TABLESPOON SRIRACHA HOT SAUCE
- 1 TABLESPOON SOY SAUCE (LIKE BRAGG® LIQUID AMINOS)

- 1 TABLESPOON MIRIN
- 1/2-INCH PIECE FRESH GINGER
- 2 TO 3 TABLESPOONS WATER

Into the work bowl of the food processor, add the peanut butter, sesame oil, rice vinegar, Sriracha, soy sauce, mirin, and ginger. Blend until smooth. Add enough water to form a thick but pourable sauce. (Makes about 3/4 cup.)

Cut the Napa cabbage in half; reserve leaves for the wraps. Cut the root end off of the cabbage and discard. Place the remaining cabbage in the food processor and pulse 5 times until finely chopped but not mushy. Place the chopped cabbage in a large bowl and set aside.

Place the mushrooms into the food processor and pulse 5 times until finely chopped. Add them to the bowl with the cabbage. Place the carrots and bell pepper in the food processor and repeat the process of pulsing 5 times. Add this to the vegetable mixture. Place the ginger and garlic in the food processor and pulse. Add this to the vegetable mixture along with the five-spice, black pepper, and salt.

Put a wok or large frying pan over the highest heat on the stovetop, and let it heat up until wisps of smoke rise up from the hot metal. Carefully pour in one tablespoon of olive oil and wait for it to start to smoke. Now, put the tofu into the wok and give it a shake—be aware that it may pop and splatter. Let the tofu rest in the hot pan without being disturbed for 45 seconds before tossing to redistribute it. Flip the tofu two additional times; after each flip, allow tofu to cook for 1 minute or until nicely browned. Remove tofu from the wok and place it into the food processor along with the peanuts. Pulse the food processor 5 times until mixture is finely chopped.

Add the remaining olive oil to the hot wok. Repeat the same stir-frying process with the vegetable mixture. Once the mixture looks dry, add the tofu and peanut mixture and toss to incorporate. Spoon mixture onto a serving platter. Garnish with cilantro leaves. Serve alongside the reserved cabbage leaves and the peanut sauce.

SPICY EDAMAME WITH TOGARASHI

We totally had one of those *Why-didn't-I think-of-that?* moments when a beautiful plate of spicy edamame arrived at our table one night at Sekisui Pacific Rim in East Memphis. While ordering our usual favorites, we noticed one of the specials: Spicy Edamame. Our server gave us one of those it's-so-good-you-have-to-order-it looks when we asked about the dish.

It was a perfectly simple mix of butter, soy sauce, Sriracha, and garlic. What a cool concept! With this version, the spices on the outside of the pod are delivered along with the bean. It's genius! These are even better than the regular old sea-salted original. We had a race to the bottom of the bowl and vowed to make them at home so you can try them too.

Serves 2.

- 1 TABLESPOON UNSALTED BUTTER
- 2 CUPS FROZEN EDAMAME (IN THE POD) (DEFROSTED)
- 1/4 TEASPOON GRANULATED GARLIC

- 1 TEASPOON SAMBAL HOT SAUCE
- 1 TEASPOON SOY SAUCE (LIKE BRAGG® LIQUID AMINOS)

- TOGARASHI (A JAPANESE SPICE MIXTURE CONTAINING ORANGE PEEL, HOT CHILIS, SEAWEED, AND SESAME SEEDS)

In a medium pan over medium heat, melt the butter and then add the edamame, garlic, and sambal. Cook for 3 to 4 minutes or until warmed through. Add the soy sauce and toss until most of the liquid has evaporated. Transfer to a plate and sprinkle with Togarashi to taste.

SANDWICHES, TACOS & MORE

. . . .

ASIAN-INSPIRED TACO BAR

While we're usually not the ones bringing the seven-layer dip, throwing down a platter of homemade wings, or baking team-color-frosted brownies, you can count on us to provide the Mexican-Korean-Japanese fusion taco bar on game day. This serve-yourself spread works well for those times when continuous grazing is key. We bet your crowd will welcome something unexpected that packs a spicy punch as y'all gather to watch, celebrate, and most importantly, eat.

Serves 8-10.

- 1 TABLESPOON OLIVE OIL
- 1 TABLESPOON TOASTED SESAME OIL
- 3 MEDIUM JAPANESE EGGPLANT (SLICED INTO HALF MOONS, ABOUT 6 CUPS)
- 1 BUNCH GREEN ONIONS (DISCARD ROOT END; RESERVE DARK GREEN TOPS FOR GARNISH)

- JUICE OF 1 LIME
- 3/4 CUP GOCHUJANG
- 1/4 CUP CHOPPED ROASTED PEANUTS (TO GARNISH)

ON THE SIDE:
- 1 ROMAINE HEART (CHOPPED)
- 1 AVOCADO (SLICED)
- 6 OUNCES KIMCHI
- 5 OUNCES QUESO FRESCO

- 2 LIMES (QUARTERED)
- 3 MINI SWEET BELL PEPPERS (THINLY SLICED)
- 1 BUNCH CILANTRO
- 3 SERRANO PEPPERS (SEARED IN A HOT PAN)
- 12 ORGANIC CORN TORTILLAS (HEATED IN A DRY SKILLET)

Put your seasoned wok or large frying pan over the highest heat on the stovetop and let it heat up until you see little wisps of smoke rise up off of the hot metal. Carefully pour in the olive and sesame oils and wait for it all to start to smoke. Now, put your eggplant and green onions in and give the pan a little shake. Let the mixture rest in the hot pan for 45 seconds before tossing everything to redistribute it by pushing the pan forward and then jerking it back just like you'd do to flip an omelette (or just use a spatula). Allow the vegetables to rest for another 45 seconds to 1 minute before flipping them again. Flip the vegetables one last time and allow them to cook for 1 minute. At this point, add your lime juice and gochujang and cook for one more minute. Remove the stir-fry from the wok and place it on a serving platter. Top it with the peanuts and reserved green onions. (The whole cooking process takes less than 4 minutes.)

Serve alongside chopped romaine hearts, sliced avocado, kimchi, queso fresco, thinly sliced mini sweet bell peppers, cilantro, and seared serrano peppers. Each guest can build his or her own masterpiece atop one of the 12 tortillas.

DO CHUA (PICKLED CARROTS AND RADISH)

- 1 MEDIUM CARROT
- 4 MEDIUM RADISHES
- 1/4 CUP WATER
- 1/4 CUP RICE VINEGAR
- 1 TEASPOON KOSHER SALT
- 1 TEASPOON HONEY

Thinly slice carrots and radishes using a mandolin or sharp knife. Place vegetables into a 1/2-pint Mason jar. In a small pan over high heat, bring the water, vinegar, salt, and honey to a boil. Remove from heat and carefully pour over the vegetables in the jar. Place the lid on the jar and store in the fridge until ready to serve. (Makes about 1 cup.)

GRILLED EGGPLANT BÁHN MÌ SANDWICH

This is just a whole bunch of awesome! Each component of this classic Vietnamese sandwich adds plenty of depth and character, so the dish as a whole is complex and amazing. One of our secrets here is adding a little cocoa powder to the Shiitake Mushroom Paté. Our friend Tuyen Le, a Vietnamese chef, urged us to try it, and we've made our paté with cocoa ever since. It's strange how savory cocoa powder is without a bunch of sugar mixed with it.

Sometimes we make this sandwich with fried eggs or pan-seared tofu in place of the eggplant, so don't feel tied to the idea of eggplant if you aren't a big fan of it. The bright pickles, crunchy cucumber, herbaceous cilantro, savory paté, and rich Sriracha mayo will play a brilliant supporting role to anything you want to throw in there.

Serves 4.

- DO CHUA (RECIPE ON PREVIOUS PAGE)
- SHIITAKE MUSHROOM PATÉ (RECIPE FOLLOWS)
- GRILLED EGGPLANT (RECIPE FOLLOWS)
- 2 12-INCH CRISPY BAGUETTES
- 1/4 CUP MAYONNAISE
- 1 TABLESPOON SRIRACHA HOT SAUCE
- 1 CUCUMBER (SLICED)
- 1 SERRANO OR JALAPEÑO PEPPER (THINLY SLICED)
- 2 GREEN ONIONS (SLICED)
- CILANTRO LEAVES (TO GARNISH)
- KOSHER SALT (TO TASTE)
- 2 MEDIUM LIMES (QUARTERED)

Preheat your oven to 350 degrees. Make the Do Choa, Shiitake Mushroom Paté, and Grilled Eggplant according to the recipes. In the oven, warm the baguettes so the outside is crispy. Split each baguette down one side and leave the other side intact (like a hinge). In a small bowl, combine the mayonnaise and Sriracha to make Sriracha mayo. Start assembling the sandwiches by spreading the Sriracha mayo on the top and the paté on the bottom. Continue by adding eggplant, cucumber, hot pepper slices, sliced green onion, Do Chua, and garnish with cilantro leaves. Add salt to taste. Cut each sandwich in half and serve with lime wedges.

continued on next page →

SHIITAKE MUSHROOM PATÉ

- 1 TABLESPOON OLIVE OIL
  (OR UNSALTED BUTTER)
- 1 TABLESPOON SESAME OIL
- 2 CUPS SLICED SHIITAKE MUSHROOMS
  (ABOUT 10 OUNCES, STEMS AND ALL)
- 1 LARGE SHALLOT, SLICED (1/2 CUP)
- 1/2 CUP WATER
- 1 TABLESPOON SOY SAUCE
  (LIKE BRAGG® LIQUID AMINOS)
- 1 TEASPOON UNSWEETENED COCOA POWDER
- CRACKED BLACK PEPPER (TO TASTE)

In a large frying pan over high heat, carefully add the olive and sesame oil. Once the oil starts to shimmer, add the shiitake mushrooms and shallots. Allow mushrooms and shallots to pick up plenty of color from the pan before stirring; this gives your paté a deep flavor. Cook mushrooms for a total of 2 minutes. Deglaze the pan with 1/2 cup water and transfer the contents of the pan to your food processor.

Add the soy sauce, cocoa powder, and pepper. Blend until very smooth. Place paté in a bowl and store in the fridge until ready to serve. (Makes about 1 cup.)

GRILLED EGGPLANT

- 1 MEDIUM EGGPLANT
- 1 TABLESPOON SOY SAUCE
  (LIKE BRAGG® LIQUID AMINOS)
- 1 TABLESPOON SESAME OIL
- 1 TABLESPOON RICE VINEGAR
- CRACKED BLACK PEPPER (TO TASTE)

Preheat your outdoor grill to high—or if a grill isn't available, use a cast-iron grill pan. Using a vegetable peeler, remove 1/2 of the eggplant skin in long strips. Slice eggplant into 1/2-inch rounds and place onto a rimmed baking sheet. In a small Mason jar or bowl, combine the soy sauce, sesame oil, and rice vinegar and mix well to emulsify. Brush both sides of each eggplant slice with the mixture and add pepper to taste.

Grill eggplant slices for 3 to 4 minutes per side or until well-marked by the grill grates. Remove and wrap slices in aluminum foil until ready to serve.

CHARRED CARROT HOT DOGS

'Char' is one of those buzzwords that's popping up on a lot of menus these days. It's completely understandable! Charring something is quite exciting. Take roasted red peppers, for example: charring the outside of the pepper renders a pliable, sweet, smoky, and delicious treat. So, why stop there? We need to be charring some other things, too, right?

What could we create with a little char? we asked ourselves. The answer came when we spied some overgrown organic carrots in the produce section: gotta do a vegetarian version of a hot dog! Once we tried it, we were hooked. The texture of the carrot is smooth and meaty, and the smoky sweetness is pronounced. All we add is salt, pepper, and touch of sesame oil. Top these dogs however you'd like: chili and cheddar with chopped white onion, mustard and sauerkraut, or ketchup and pickle relish.

Serves 4.

- 6 VERY LARGE CARROTS
- 1 TEASPOON TOASTED SESAME OIL
- KOSHER SALT AND CRACKED BLACK PEPPER (TO TASTE)

- 6 WHOLE WHEAT HOT DOG BUNS
- TOPPING OPTIONS: VEGETARIAN CHILI, CHEDDAR, CHOPPED ONION,

SAUERKRAUT, PICKLES, KETCHUP, SPICY MUSTARD (TO SERVE)

Over a high flame on your outdoor grill's side burner or under your oven's broiler, char the carrots until they are deeply blackened all over. This will take roughly 20 minutes if you give the carrots a quarter turn every 5 minutes. Once they are sufficiently blackened, remove them and wrap them tightly in aluminum foil. Allow the charred carrots to rest for 15 minutes. They will finish cooking through during that time, and a smoky flavor will infuse throughout.

When the carrots are cool enough to handle, pull the char off of each carrot just like you would for a roasted red pepper. Drizzle the carrots with sesame oil and add salt and pepper to taste. Feel free to warm them up on the grill if you'd like. Serve them on a bun with your favorite toppings.

NOTE: Look for the carrots that are about as big around as a half-dollar and have very little taper to them. The biggest carrots you can find are what's going to work best here. They shrink slightly during the cooking process, and then you pull off the charred part, so they will be smaller once it comes time to eat them.

SPRING ROLL WRAP WITH SPICY SRIRACHA PEANUT SAUCE

What's the only downside of a delicious spring roll? It's definitely the fact that they're so very small. When we crave Vietnamese food, we each get an order of spring rolls because they're just too good to have to share. We love them stuffed with noodles, seared tofu, avocado, and tons of fresh herbs like mint, basil, and green onions. At home, we like to make meal-sized spring rolls by wrapping all the same tasty ingredients up in a brown rice tortilla. Tons of fresh herbs and our Spicy Sriracha Peanut Sauce make these rock.

Serves 4.

- 1 TABLESPOON VEGETABLE OIL
- 1 PACKAGE FIRM TOFU (SLICED INTO 12 PIECES, PATTED DRY)
- 1/2 TEASPOON KOSHER SALT
- 1/2 TEASPOON CRACKED BLACK PEPPER
- SPICY SRIRACHA PEANUT SAUCE (RECIPE FOLLOWS)

- 1 1/2 CUPS BEAN THREAD NOODLES (PREPARED ACCORDING TO PACKAGE DIRECTIONS)
- 4 BROWN RICE TORTILLAS
- 1 1/2 CUPS SHREDDED ICEBERG LETTUCE
- 1 LARGE AVOCADO (PEELED, SLICED)

- 1 MEDIUM CARROT (JULIENNED)
- 1 SMALL CUCUMBER (THINLY SLICED)
- 1 CUP FRESH CILANTRO LEAVES
- 1 CUP FRESH MINT LEAVES
- 1 CUP FRESH BASIL LEAVES
- 2 GREEN ONIONS (SLICED)

In a large frying pan over high heat, add the oil. Once it starts smoking, carefully slide the tofu slices into the pan. Be careful, they will splatter if not completely dry. (Know that dry tofu and a hot pan assure that the tofu won't stick.) Season the side of the tofu facing up with salt and pepper and allow it to cook for 1 1/2 to 2 minutes or until nicely browned. Flip tofu and cook for another 2 to 3 minutes or until browned. Remove tofu from the pan and set aside.

Prepare the Spicy Sriracha Peanut Sauce and bean thread noodles according to the instructions. Heat the tortillas in a dry pan until soft and pliable.

Assemble the Spring Roll Wrap by dividing the noodles, lettuce, avocado, carrot, cucumber, cilantro, mint, basil, green onions, and tofu among the tortillas and drizzle each with Spicy Sriracha Peanut Sauce.

NOTE: Bean thread noodles are available at Asian markets and at some grocery stores. They are also sometimes called cellophane noodles. Just look for the thin, clear, bean noodles or use rice noodles in their place.

SPICY SRIRACHA PEANUT SAUCE

- 2 TABLESPOONS PEANUT BUTTER
- 2 TABLESPOONS MIRIN
- 2 TABLESPOONS SOY SAUCE
  (LIKE BRAGG® LIQUID AMINOS)
- 2 TABLESPOONS SRIRACHA HOT SAUCE
- 1 CLOVE GARLIC

Using an immersion blender or food processor, blend the peanut butter, mirin, soy sauce, Sriracha, and garlic until smooth. Add enough water to get a pourable but still thick consistency. (Makes about 1/2 cup.)

In a stock pot over medium heat, add the olive oil and heat until it starts to shimmer. Add the onions, celery, and carrots and cook until it's all nice and brown. This takes about 20 minutes with some occasional stirring, but it's worth it. The flavor gained from all those brown bits is amazing!

Add the garlic, thyme, porcini, bay leaves, and red wine to the pot. Scrape up any bits that are stuck to the bottom of the pot, and cook until it looks dry, about 10 minutes. Add the stock, sliced portobellos, vinegar, tomato paste, and Worcestershire. Once the liquid starts to simmer, reduce to low heat, and cook, uncovered, for 45 minutes. The liquid should have reduced significantly by the end of the cooking time. Serve heaped onto French rolls and garnish with pickles, sliced tomatoes, mayonnaise, Creole mustard, and lettuce.

THE CHUBBY VEGETARIAN DEBRIS PO' BOY AT THE SECOND LINE

We're super-pumped to be a part of the po' boy menu at Chef Kelly English's Memphis restaurant, The Second Line. It all stared with a conversation: "I've never had a po' boy that was intended to be vegetarian, but still rang true," Chef English told us. "I don't want it to be so gussied up that it no longer resembles a po' boy," he continued. "So that's exactly what I want, and I know you're up to the task!"

We don't want to oversell this sandwich, but it really is amazing! Fresh portobello or crimini mushrooms are braised in red wine with celery, carrots, garlic, thyme, and bay leaves. The mushrooms form their own flavorful broth during the braise, which is then spooned generously onto a baguette and garnished with pickles, lettuce, tomato, and mayo.

"A po' boy has to drip down your arm with the first bite," Kelly is fond of saying. So we wanted to deliver just that. It's a wonderfully messy thing! "What we ended up with," he said, "I couldn't be prouder of, and it's one of the first recommendations I make, to any type of 'vore: carnivore, herbivore, or omnivore."

Serves 6.

- 2 TABLESPOONS OLIVE OIL
- 1 LARGE WHITE ONION (THINLY SLICED INTO HALF-MOONS)
- 2 MEDIUM RIBS CELERY (THINLY SLICED)
- 2 MEDIUM CARROTS (THINLY SLICED)
- 6 CLOVES GARLIC (SMASHED)
- 1 TEASPOON DRIED THYME
- 1 TABLESPOON DRIED, CRUMBLED PORCINI MUSHROOMS
- 2 BAY LEAVES
- 1 1/2 CUPS DRY RED WINE
- 2 CUPS VEGETABLE STOCK
- 4 TO 5 LARGE PORTOBELLO MUSHROOMS OR 3 8-OUNCE PACKAGES OF CRIMINI MUSHROOMS (THINLY SLICED)
- 1 TABLESPOON CHAMPAGNE VINEGAR
- 1 HEAPING TABLESPOON TOMATO PASTE
- 1 TABLESPOON VEGETARIAN WORCESTERSHIRE
- HOT SAUCE (TO TASTE)
- 3 12-INCH CRISPY FRENCH ROLLS (SPLIT)
- PICKLES, SLICED TOMATOES, MAYONNAISE (VEGAN OR REGULAR), CREOLE MUSTARD, AND THINLY SLICED ICEBERG LETTUCE (TO GARNISH)

PURPLE CABBAGE SLAW

- 2 CUPS GRATED PURPLE CABBAGE
  (ABOUT 1/2 OF A MEDIUM HEAD)
- JUICE OF 1 LIME
- 1 TEASPOON SUGAR
- 1/4 CUP SOUR CREAM

- KOSHER SALT AND CRACKED
  BLACK PEPPER (TO TASTE)

In a large bowl, mix the cabbage, lime juice, sugar, sour cream, salt, and pepper together until well-incorporated. (Makes about 1 1/2 cups.)

CRISPY BAKED AVOCADO TACOS WITH PURPLE CABBAGE SLAW

When you're selecting avocados for this dish, look for ones that are just ripe and still a little firm. You'll have a pretty hard time working with an avocado that's too soft. Also look for the Haas variety with the dark, pebbly skin. The smooth, lighter green avocados contain too much water to be used in this recipe.

These would be just as good (read: maybe even better?) pan-fried—or dare we say it, deep-fried!—but as always, we looked for a balance of flavor and fat. The panko bread crumbs give the avocado a satisfying crunch without the involvement of a deep fryer.

Makes 8 tacos; serves 4.

- 1/2 CUP ALL-PURPOSE FLOUR
- 1/4 TEASPOON KOSHER SALT
- 1/4 TEASPOON GRANULATED GARLIC
- 1/4 TEASPOON GROUND SAGE
- 1/4 TEASPOON CRACKED BLACK PEPPER

- 1 LARGE EGG (BEATEN)
- 1/4 CUP WATER
- 1/2 CUP PANKO BREAD CRUMBS
- 2 LARGE HAAS AVOCADOS (PEELED AND QUARTERED)
- 1 1/2 TABLESPOONS VEGETABLE OIL

- 8 SMALL CORN OR FLOUR TORTILLAS
- PURPLE CABBAGE SLAW (RECIPE ON PREVIOUS PAGE)
- RED ONION (SLICED), COTIJA CHEESE, HOT SAUCE (TO GARNISH)

Preheat your oven to 425 degrees. Set up a 3-bowl system for coating the avocado quarters. In the first bowl, mix the all-purpose flour, salt, granulated garlic, sage, and pepper. The second bowl should have the beaten egg and the water mixed until smooth. The last bowl should have the panko bread crumbs.

Dip each avocado quarter into the flour, and then the egg, and then the panko to coat. Place them on a parchment-lined baking sheet. Once all quarters are coated, drizzle them with the vegetable oil and place them in the oven for 20 to 25 minutes, turning them halfway through, or until they're nicely browned.

Serve in tortillas with a scoop of Purple Cabbage Slaw, red onion, crumbled cotija cheese, and your favorite Mexican hot sauce.

VEGAN CHIPOTLE SWEET POTATO BURGER

This is another one of our occasional attempts at really easy and delicious veggie burgers. The truth is, if you add equal parts of quick-cooking oats to mashed beans or sweet potatoes or squash (or whatever), it'll yield a workable mixture that is well-suited to be formed into a burger patty. All you need to do from that point is add a little seasoning.

Just to be clear, these are not the kind of burgers that are meant to taste like ground beef. We're not huge fans of that type of thing. These particular burgers taste like roasted sweet potato, smoked chilies, and cumin. It's a great combination of smoky, spicy, and sweet—especially paired with rich slices of avocado and some tangy salsa.

Serves 4.

- 1 1/2 CUPS BAKED, PEELED, MASHED SWEET POTATO (1 LARGE OR 2 MEDIUM)
- 1 1/2 CUPS QUICK-COOKING OATS
- 1/2 TEASPOON CUMIN
- 1/4 TEASPOON GRANULATED GARLIC
- 1/4 TEASPOON KOSHER SALT
- 1/4 TEASPOON CRACKED BLACK PEPPER
- 1 OR 2 MINCED CHIPOTLE CHILIES (FROM A CAN)
- VEGETABLE OIL (FOR PAN-FRYING)
- 4 KAISER ROLLS
- AVOCADO SLICES, TOMATO SLICES, ARUGULA, AND SALSA (TO GARNISH)

In a large bowl, mix the mashed sweet potato, oats, cumin, garlic, salt, pepper, and chipotles until well-incorporated. Cover and set aside in the fridge for 15 minutes to allow the moisture to distribute. Form the mixture into 4 patties and pan-fry over medium heat in oil for about 4 minutes per side. Serve on a Kaiser roll with slices of avocado, tomato, arugula, and salsa.

FRENCH ONION GRILLED CHEESE

French onion soup has ruined so many articles of clothing since its invention. Usually, we can't wait to dig in, and as soon as we press our spoons into the gooey cheese, the hot broth jumps out, and there goes yet another new or favorite shirt. Well, now we can all put our makeshift French onion soup bibs away! We've created a safer, cuter French onion grilled cheese sandwich. It's a mix of the soup you remember and the grilled cheese you've always loved.

Serves 4.

- 4 LARGE WHITE OR YELLOW ONIONS (THINLY SLICED, ABOUT 7 CUPS)
- 3 TABLESPOONS UNSALTED BUTTER (DIVIDED)
- 1 CUP RED WINE
- 1/4 TEASPOON CRACKED BLACK PEPPER
- 1 TABLESPOON VEGETARIAN WORCESTERSHIRE SAUCE
- 1 TEASPOON SHERRY VINEGAR
- 5 SPRIGS FRESH THYME
- 1/2 TEASPOON GRANULATED GARLIC
- 2 BAY LEAVES
- 2 TEASPOONS SOY SAUCE (LIKE BRAGG® LIQUID AMINOS)
- 1 QUART VEGETABLE BROTH
- 8 OUNCES GRUYÈRE CHEESE (SHREDDED)
- 8 SLICES BREAD

In a large soup pot or Dutch oven, layer in the onions and 2 tablespoons of the butter. Cover and set the heat to low for about 20 minutes. Remove the cover and raise the heat to medium. Continue to cook and occasionally stir until the onions are deeply browned, which will take another 20 minutes. Deglaze the pan with the red wine; make sure to scrape up any bits that are stuck to the bottom. Increase the heat and reduce the wine by half. Now add the pepper, Worcestershire, vinegar, thyme, granulated garlic, bay leaves, soy sauce, and vegetable broth to the pot. Stir to incorporate, bring to a simmer, cover, and reduce the heat. Allow mixture to cook for 20 to 30 minutes so that the flavors meld.

Strain the soup through a fine mesh sieve and fish out the bay leaves and thyme stems. Return the broth to the soup pot in order to keep it warm.

Assemble the grilled cheese sandwiches by adding 1/3 cup of grated gruyère and 1/3 cup of the onion mixture each onto 4 slices of bread. Top with remaining bread slices. Add the remaining tablespoon of butter to a large frying pan and melt the butter over medium heat. Grill the sandwiches for about 3 minutes per side or until the bread is golden brown and the cheese has melted. Serve the grilled cheese with a cup of warm broth for dipping.

ITALIAN-STYLE EGGPLANT SAUSAGES

Why not make a vegetarian sausage out of a vegetable that has a meaty texture and is already pretty much shaped like a sausage? We're talking about Japanese eggplant, of course. They're often available at specialty grocery stores, but if the one near you doesn't carry them, they can easily be found year-round at most Asian markets.

Here, we've flavored the Japanese eggplants using the same spice blend you'd find in almost any Italian sausage. It's a savory mix of sage, fennel, and spice. We serve them like they do in Jersey: hot-dog style on a hoagie roll, with potatoes, peppers, onions, and plenty of mustard.

Serves 6.

- 1/4 CUP OLIVE OIL
- 6 12-INCH LONG JAPANESE EGGPLANTS (PEELED USING A VEGETABLE PEELER)
- 1 TEASPOON GROUND FENNEL (OR FENNEL POLLEN)
- 1 TEASPOON RED PEPPER FLAKES
- 1 TEASPOON RUBBED SAGE

- 1 TEASPOON ITALIAN SEASONING
- 2 TEASPOONS KOSHER SALT
- 1/2 TEASPOON CRACKED BLACK PEPPER
- 1/2 TEASPOON ONION POWDER
- 1/2 TEASPOON GARLIC POWDER

- 6 12-INCH HOAGIE ROLLS (LIGHT AND CRISP LIKE FRENCH BREAD)
- MUSTARD (TO GARNISH)
- POTATO, ONION, AND PEPPER TOPPING (RECIPE FOLLOWS)
- 1 CUP SHREDDED MOZZARELLA (OPTIONAL)

Into a large bowl, pour olive oil over the peeled eggplants and rub it in so that the oil is absorbed. In a small bowl, make a spice mixture using the fennel, red pepper flakes, sage, Italian seasoning, salt, pepper, onion powder, and garlic powder. Generously rub each eggplant with the spice mixture. (You should use all the spice mixture for this.) Place the eggplants in a plastic bag in the refrigerator to marinate for at least an hour or even overnight.

Cook the eggplants over medium heat using a cast-iron grill pan. Cook for 3 to 4 minutes per side or until well-marked by the grill grates. Cook for a total of 12 to 16 minutes or until heated through. Serve on warm hoagie rolls that have been slathered with mustard and stuffed with the Potato, Onion, and Pepper Topping. Add cheese to the top of each and melt it under the broiler if you wish.

POTATO, ONION, AND PEPPER TOPPING

- 2 TABLESPOONS VEGETABLE OIL
- 1 MEDIUM POTATO (PEELED, DICED)
- 1 ONION (PEELED, DICED)
- 1 GREEN PEPPER (DICED)
- 1 TABLESPOON TOMATO PASTE
- KOSHER SALT AND CRACKED BLACK PEPPER (TO TASTE)

In a large frying pan over medium-high heat, add the oil and wait for it to shimmer. Carefully add the potato, onion, and green pepper in a single layer. Allow mixture to cook undisturbed for about 3 minutes or until nicely browned. Toss in the tomato paste and cook until potatoes are tender, for about another 3 minutes. Remove from heat, season with salt and pepper, cover, and set aside until ready to assemble. (Makes about 2 cups.)

MAIN DISHES

. . . .

continued on next page →

MAIN DISHES

· ·

CHIPOTLE ENCHILADA SAUCE

- 1 28-OUNCE CAN DICED FIRE-ROASTED TOMATOES
- 1 CLOVE GARLIC
- 1 CHIPOTLE PEPPER (FROM A CAN)
- 1 TEASPOON SHERRY VINEGAR

Into a blender or food processor, place the tomatoes, garlic, chipotle pepper, and sherry vinegar. Blend until smooth. In a saucepan over medium heat, warm the Chipotle Enchilada Sauce through and then turn off the heat. This can be made ahead of time and refrigerated up to 5 days or frozen up to 6 months. (Makes 3 1/2 cups.)

SWEET POTATO, KALE, AND BLACK BEAN ENCHILADAS

Enchiladas are easily a once-a-week meal at our house, so it's strange that during the first eight years we'd been writing The Chubby Vegetarian blog, we'd never shared a single recipe for them. That may be a good thing, though, because over the years, we've simplified the process and amplified the flavor. The cool thing is that this recipe makes a ton, so you're sure to have leftovers (which is kind of our favorite part).

Serves 4.

- CHIPOTLE ENCHILADA SAUCE (RECIPE ON PREVIOUS PAGE)
- 1 TABLESPOON OLIVE OIL
- 1 MEDIUM SWEET POTATO (PEELED AND DICED, ABOUT 2 CUPS)
- 1/2 MEDIUM RED ONION (DICED, ABOUT 1 CUP)
- 2 HEAPING CUPS DE-STEMMED, FINELY CHOPPED KALE
- 1 TEASPOON CUMIN
- 1 15-OUNCE CAN BLACK BEANS
- 1 TEASPOON SHERRY VINEGAR
- KOSHER SALT AND CRACKED BLACK PEPPER (TO TASTE)
- 8 SMALL CORN OR FLOUR TORTILLAS (WARMED)
- 2 CUPS SHREDDED CHEDDAR CHEESE
- OPTIONAL TOPPINGS: GREEK YOGURT, CHOPPED AVOCADO, CILANTRO, SLICED RADISH, CHOPPED GREEN ONION, AND HOT SAUCE

Make Chipotle Enchilada Sauce according to the recipe and keep warm in a saucepan until ready to assemble the enchiladas. In a large skillet over medium heat, add the olive oil and the diced sweet potato. Cook, stirring often, until the sweet potato has softened and is beginning to brown (about 10 minutes). Add the onion and cook until it starts to soften. This will take about 5 minutes. Add the kale, cumin, black beans, and vinegar. Season with salt and pepper to taste. Stir and cover until sauce is heated through and the kale has wilted (about 6 minutes).

Preheat your oven to 350 degrees. Into a 9 x 12-inch casserole dish, add 3/4 cup of Chipotle Enchilada Sauce and spread it around the bottom in a thin layer.

Lay the tortillas out on the counter and divide 1 1/2 cups of the cheese among them while reserving the rest to sprinkle on top. Divide the filling among the tortillas; each tortilla will need about 1/4 cup. Roll the tortillas and place seam-side-down into the casserole dish. Repeat until all tortillas are wrapped. Top with the remaining Chipotle Enchilada Sauce and cheese. Bake for 20 minutes or until the sauce is bubbling and the cheese has melted.

Serve topped however you'd like; we usually have some combination of the ingredients in the 'Optional Toppings' listed above in the recipe. Place the leftovers in a lidded container and freeze them for an easy and delicious weeknight dinner.

7-LAYER CHIPOTLE-CHOCOLATE CHILI

The most common question that's asked when the subject of vegetarianism comes up is definitely this one: "So, where do you get your protein?" The question is asked with a slight tilt of the head and an abundance of concern as if the person is trying to figure out how you're standing upright with, he or she figures, no protein at all in your diet. Well, believe it or not, many plant-based foods, particularly seeds, nuts, and grains, are great sources of protein, and there are benefits to getting at least some of your protein from vegetable sources.

This dish uses quinoa, a complete protein, as its base and is topped with a protein-packed chili that's made using lentils and walnuts. The depth of flavor comes from two sources: smoky chipotle chili peppers and dark chocolate. This chili is so easy to make—you seriously won't believe it—since there's no sautéing and almost no chopping.

Serves 4.

- 1 16-OUNCE JAR FIRE-ROASTED SALSA
- 1 CUP DRIED GREEN LENTILS
- 2 CUPS VEGETABLE STOCK
- 1 CUP WATER
- 1/2 CUP CHOPPED RAW WALNUTS

- 1 CHIPOTLE CHILI FROM A CAN (MINCED)
- 1 OUNCE 72% DARK CHOCOLATE
- 1 TEASPOON CUMIN
- CORIANDER QUINOA (RECIPE FOLLOWS)

- CHERRY TOMATO PICO DE GALLO (RECIPE FOLLOWS)
- NO-FUSS GUACAMOLE (RECIPE FOLLOWS)
- 4 OUNCES SHREDDED CHEDDAR CHEESE
- 2 CUPS SHREDDED LETTUCE
- 1 CUP GREEK YOGURT

Into a medium saucepan over medium-high heat, add the salsa, lentils, vegetable stock, water, walnuts, chipotle, chocolate, and cumin. Cover and bring to a boil. Reduce mixture to a simmer for 40 minutes or until lentils are tender. (Most of the liquid will be absorbed by the lentils.)

While the chili cooks, make the Coriander Quinoa, Cherry Tomato Pico De Gallo, and No-Fuss Guacamole. Assemble each serving by adding 1/2 cup of Coriander Quinoa to a medium bowl and top it with 3/4 cup of the 7-Layer Chipotle-Chocolate Chili. Layer one quarter each of the cheese, lettuce, yogurt, and No-Fuss Guacamole. Finally, top it all off with 1/4 cup Cherry Tomato Pico de Gallo. Repeat the same pattern in the next 3 bowls.

continued on next page →

CORIANDER QUINOA

- 2 CUPS VEGETABLE STOCK
- 1 CUP WHITE QUINOA
  (RINSED UNDER COLD WATER)
- 1 TEASPOON CORIANDER

Into a medium saucepan over high heat, bring the stock to a boil and add the quinoa and coriander. Cover and reduce to a simmer for 20 minutes. Uncover and fluff with a fork. (Makes about 2 1/2 cups.)

CHERRY TOMATO PICO DE GALLO

- 1 SMALL SHALLOT (FINELY DICED)
- 1 PINT CHERRY TOMATOES (HALVED)
- 1 CUP CILANTRO LEAVES
- JUICE OF 1 LIME
- 1 SMALL SERRANO PEPPER (FINELY DICED)
- KOSHER SALT AND CRACKED BLACK PEPPER
  (TO TASTE)

Rinse the diced shallot under cold water. (This will keep the onion from overpowering the mixture.) In a medium bowl, combine the shallot, tomatoes, cilantro, lime juice, and Serrano pepper. Add salt and pepper to taste. (Makes about 2 cups.)

NO-FUSS GUACAMOLE

- 2 RIPE MEDIUM-SIZED HAAS AVOCADOS
- JUICE FROM 1 ORANGE
- 1/8 TEASPOON SUGAR (OPTIONAL)
- 1 TEASPOON OLIVE OIL
- KOSHER SALT AND CRACKED BLACK PEPPER
  (TO TASTE)

Peel and dice the avocados and place them in a medium bowl. Add the orange juice, sugar, olive oil, salt, and pepper and stir. (Makes about 1 1/2 cups.)

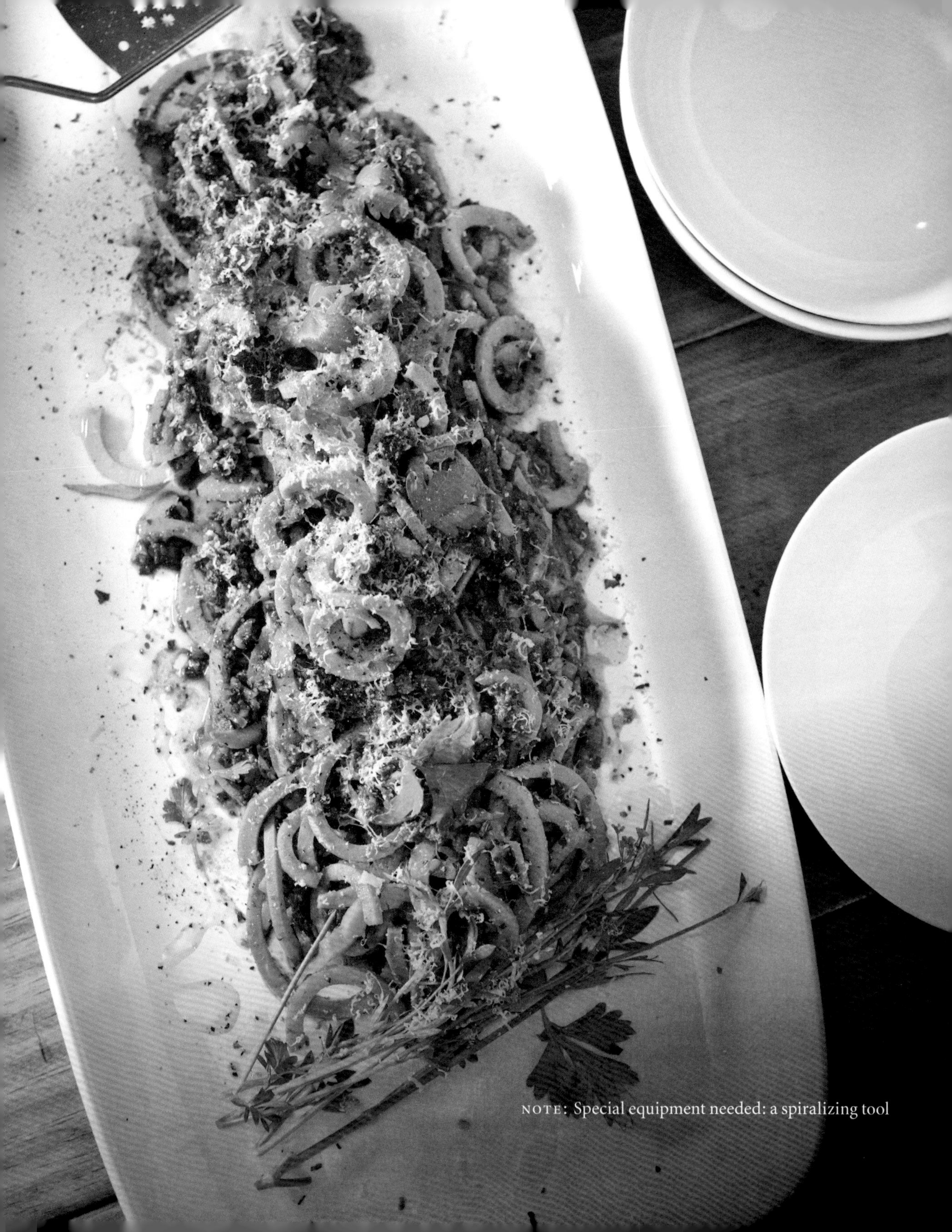

NOTE: Special equipment needed: a spiralizing tool

SPIRALIZED SWEET POTATO NOODLES WITH MUSHROOM BOLOGNESE SAUCE

This particular recipe was helpful to us in making the jump to all-veg, no-starch "pasta" for dinner...well, sometimes, at least! It's real comfort food made with whole ingredients; it may even impress the folks who think they'll miss the taste, texture, or really the entire experience of traditional pasta. The sauce highlights deep, rich flavors, and the sweet potato noodles are surprisingly good.

(If you've been a bit skeptical about this whole spiralizing idea, do what we did at first: mix in some traditional pasta with spirialized sweet potatoes, carrots, or zucchini. We think you'll love how it lightens up your usual pasta plate.)

Serves 4.

- 1 CUP CHOPPED ONION
- 1/2 CUP PEELED GARLIC CLOVES
- 1/4 CUP OLIVE OIL
- 2 CUPS CHOPPED PORTOBELLO MUSHROOMS
- 1 TEASPOON TRUFFLE SALT (OR KOSHER SALT)
- CRACKED BLACK PEPPER (TO TASTE)
- 1 TEASPOON DRIED THYME
- 1 28-OUNCE CAN CRUSHED, FIRE-ROASTED TOMATOES
- 1 TABLESPOON BALSAMIC VINEGAR (PLUS MORE FOR GARNISH)
- 1 LARGE PEELED SWEET POTATO
- 1/4 CUP PARSLEY LEAVES (TO GARNISH)
- 1/8 CUP SHREDDED ASIAGO CHEESE (TO GARNISH)

Into the work bowl of your food processor, place the onion and the garlic. Pulse until finely chopped. Set the chopped onion and garlic mixture aside. Place the portobellos in the food processor and pulse until finely chopped. Set the mushrooms aside.

In a 12-inch skillet over medium-high heat, heat the olive oil until it shimmers. Place the finely chopped onion and garlic mixture into the pan with the olive oil. Stir the mixture and watch it carefully so that the garlic doesn't burn. Cook for 2 to 3 minutes or until the mixture starts to brown. Add the finely chopped mushrooms and cook, stirring often, until most of the liquid has evaporated from the mixture; this takes about 5 minutes. Add the truffle salt, pepper, dried thyme, tomatoes, and balsamic vinegar. Stir and reduce heat to low. Keep warm on the stovetop until ready to serve.

Bring a large pot of salted water to a boil. Spiralize the sweet potato using the largest set of blades for thick, hearty sweet potato noodles. Briefly blanch the sweet potato noodles in the salted water for 30 seconds. Remove the noodles from water and place them into the skillet containing the Mushroom Bolognese Sauce. Toss to coat. Place the mixture on a large platter and garnish with parsley leaves and shredded Asiago cheese. Drizzle the finished dish with a teaspoon of balsamic vinegar.

GRILLED SUMMER VEGETABLE PIZZA ON AN OLIVE OIL AND SPROUTED WHOLE WHEAT CRUST

Since we're always trying to figure out appealing ways to sneak more vegetables into every meal, we like to highlight early summer favorites such as Japanese eggplant, zucchini, spring onions, mini bell peppers, and baby bella mushrooms. Get some good grill marks on all of these thickly sliced beauties, and they'll be amazing toppings for this pizza.

If you've never made a crust from scratch before, this is your chance. You don't have to proof it overnight or toss it in the air like a pizzolo. The first step is drizzling a generous amount of olive oil into your skillet; this helps to ensure that your crust will be crispy and airy. Soon, it all comes together in a heathy and satisfying meal that eats like comfort food, but provides great nutrition. Isn't that the combo we all want more of in our lives?

Serves 2-4.

- 1 SPROUTED WHOLE WHEAT PIZZA CRUST (RECIPE FOLLOWS)
- 2 TABLESPOONS OLIVE OIL (DIVIDED)
- 5 LARGE BABY BELLA MUSHROOMS
- 1 SMALL JAPANESE EGGPLANT (SLICED INTO 1/2-INCH ROUNDS)

- 3 MINI RED BELL PEPPERS (HALVED, SEEDED)
- 1 SMALL ZUCCHINI SQUASH (SLICED INTO 1/2-INCH ROUNDS)
- 1 SPRING ONION (HALVED)
- 1 TABLESPOON BALSAMIC VINEGAR
- 1 TEASPOON ITALIAN SEASONING

- 1/2 TEASPOON KOSHER SALT
- 1 CUP TOMATO SAUCE
- 1 CUP LOOSE-PACKED, SHREDDED MOZZARELLA CHEESE
- FRESH PARSLEY LEAVES AND CRUSHED RED PEPPER (FOR GARNISH)

SPROUTED WHOLE WHEAT PIZZA CRUST

- 1 CUP SPROUTED WHOLE WHEAT FLOUR
- 1 TEASPOON RAPID-RISE YEAST
- 1/2 TEASPOON KOSHER SALT
- 1/2 CUP WATER

In a large mixing bowl, combine the flour, yeast, salt, and water. Mix until all four are incorporated. Cover and set aside.

Preheat your oven to 500 degrees. Make the Sprouted Whole Wheat Pizza Crust according to the recipe. Add 1 tablespoon of the olive oil to your 11-and-3/4-inch cast-iron skillet. Add the pizza dough and press it into a circle to fill the pan. Cover with plastic wrap and set aside to allow the dough to rise.

Preheat your cast-iron 15-and-3/4-inch extra-large grill or grill pan to medium. In a large mixing bowl, toss the cut vegetables with the remaining tablespoon of olive oil, balsamic vinegar, Italian seasoning, and salt. Grill the vegetables for 4 minutes per side or until well-marked by the grill grates. Remove and set aside until you're ready to assemble your pizza. At this point, slice the cooled peppers and onions into bite-sized pieces.

Assemble your pizza by removing the plastic wrap from your cast-iron pan with the crust in it and spread the tomato sauce on top of it in an even layer. Next, layer in your grilled vegetables followed by the cheese. Place the pan into the preheated oven for 20 minutes or until hot and bubbly. Carefully remove the pan and let it cool for at least 5 minutes; the pizza will be very hot in the middle. If you like, garnish pizza with fresh parsley leaves and crushed red pepper. Slice into 4 large pieces.

NOTE: One of our favorite substitutes for traditional white flour is sprouted whole wheat flour, which we use here. Feel free to make this crust with whole wheat flour if that is the option that's available in your kitchen.

ROAST BEAST

For this main dish, which we've dubbed Roast Beast, we took inspiration from the infamous turducken. *What in the world would be a vegetable version of that be like?* we pondered. What we came up with is a giant and flavorful stack of eggplant, portobello mushrooms, roasted red peppers, onions, provolone, and pesto with a dramatic presentation that'll steal the show at Thanksgiving.

Serves 4-6 as a main dish.

- 2 LARGE RED BELL PEPPERS (ROASTED AND PEELED)
- 1/2 CUP OLIVE OIL
- 1 HEAD GARLIC (PEELED, ABOUT 10 CLOVES, SMASHED)
- 1/4 CUP TOASTED PINE NUTS
- 2 CUPS PARSLEY (ABOUT ONE BUNCH)
- 1/4 CUP CHAMPAGNE VINEGAR
- 4 LARGE PORTOBELLO MUSHROOMS
- 1 MEDIUM ITALIAN EGGPLANT (SLICED INTO 1/2-INCH ROUNDS)
- KOSHER SALT AND CRACKED BLACK PEPPER (TO TASTE)
- 1 LARGE WHITE ONION
- 4 SLICES OF PROVOLONE CHEESE
- 1 1/2 CUPS COOKED ORZO OR COUSCOUS
- BALSAMIC VINEGAR (FOR DRIZZLING)

Preheat your outdoor grill to high. Prepare the roasted red peppers by charring the skins, letting them rest, and then peeling and seeding them. Set aside until ready to assemble the dish.

In a small frying pan over the grill grates (or on your side burner), heat the olive oil and add the smashed garlic. Cook until just browned. Into the work bowl of your food processor, add the olive oil, garlic, pine nuts, parsley, and vinegar. To make the pesto, process ingredients until well-incorporated, but still a little chunky. In a large bowl, toss the portobello and eggplant in with the pesto until well-coated. Reserve the pesto left in the bottom of the bowl.

Add salt and pepper to taste to all ingredients. Thread the vegetables onto a skewer: start with a mushroom and then add a slice of eggplant, half of a roasted red pepper, a slice of provolone, and a slice of onion. (You basically will be making a giant kabob.) Repeat this pattern four times. Press the stack tightly together and pierce it all at an angle with the two other skewers.

Grill on a rack positioned slightly above the grill grates for 40 minutes and turn every 10 minutes. Some of the cheese will drip out, but that's fine. Much of it will melt into the vegetables and add a ton of flavor!

Remove the Roast Beast and allow it to rest for 10 minutes while tented in foil. Serve on top of a bed of orzo or couscous. Drizzle with the leftover pesto and some balsamic vinegar.

NOTE: Special equipment needed: 3 large metal skewers

EGG FOO YUNG WITH SRIRACHA GRAVY

This is a simple recipe that we make all the time at home. It's really versatile in that you can use any mix of vegetables that you have on hand, and it's one of those dishes that you can make for breakfast, lunch, or dinner—it really works well for all three. And it's really fast! Once you've made it a few times, you can go from realizing you're hungry to eating a home-cooked meal in 10 minutes.

(We love our ceramic non-stick pans for cooking eggs this way. You should chuck your old non-stick cookware and give ceramic frying pans a try. They're slick and nothing sticks to them.)

Serves 2.

- 1 1/2 CUPS 1/4-INCH SLICED MIXED VEGETABLES (PAGE 161)
- 4 LARGE EGGS
- 3 GREEN ONIONS
- 1/8 TEASPOON GRANULATED GARLIC
- 1/8 TEASPOON GROUND GINGER
- 1/4 TEASPOON CHINESE FIVE-SPICE
- 1/4 TEASPOON KOSHER SALT
- 1/4 CRACKED BLACK PEPPER
- 2 TABLESPOONS OLIVE OIL
- SRIRACHA GRAVY (RECIPE FOLLOWS)

Using a food processor, pulse the vegetable mixture several times until it's finely chopped. Crack the eggs into a large mixing bowl and whisk them. Add the finely chopped vegetable mixture. Thinly slice the green onions and add the white part to the egg mixture; reserve the green tops for garnish. Add the garlic, ginger, five spice, salt, and pepper to the egg mixture.

In a small, 8-inch, non-stick frying pan over high heat, add 1 tablespoon of the olive oil and wait until it shimmers. Add half of the vegetable and egg mixture (about 1 cup) and allow it to cook for 1 to 2 minutes. All the while, shake the pan so that the eggs don't stick. Once the eggs brown and start to set, flip the

Egg Foo Yung and cook the other side for 1 to 2 minutes or until cooked through. Set aside and repeat with the remaining oil and egg mixture. Once you've finished both, use the pan to make the gravy.

To serve, slice Egg Foo Yung into quarters and garnish with warm Sriracha Gravy and green onion.

SRIRACHA GRAVY

- 1 TABLESPOON SOY SAUCE
  (LIKE BRAGG® LIQUID AMINOS)
- 1 TABLESPOON SRIRACHA HOT SAUCE
- 1 TEASPOON RICE VINEGAR
- 1 TEASPOON CORNSTARCH
- 1/2 CUP WATER

Place the soy sauce, Sriracha, vinegar, cornstarch, and water in a Mason jar with a lid and shake until the cornstarch has dissolved. In a 8-inch frying pan over high heat, cook the mixture until it thickens. This will take about 2 minutes. Set aside until ready to serve. (Makes about 2/3 cup of gravy.)

CAULIFLOWER IN TOMATO SAUCE WITH PINE NUTS AND PARSLEY

This is our go-to dinner when we're attempting to follow a low-carb, low-fat diet. It's fast, simple, and best of all, it's super delicious. It looks and tastes like a big helping of pasta, but it's packed with nutrition.

The secret here is going to be the sauce that you use. Just like regular pasta, the cauliflower is a vehicle for the sauce, so use one you really like. Feel free to gussy up this dish with an assortment of toppings like chopped rosemary or roasted mushrooms. It's a great stage for showcasing almost any flavor.

Serves 2.

- HALF OF A LARGE HEAD OF CAULIFLOWER
- 1 1/2 CUPS TOMATO SAUCE
- 1/4 CUP TOASTED PINE NUTS (TO GARNISH)
- 1/4 CUP PARSLEY LEAVES (TO GARNISH)
- PARMESAN CHEESE (TO GARNISH)
- KOSHER SALT AND CRACKED BLACK PEPPER (TO TASTE)

Bring a large pot of salted water to a boil; the water should be as salty as the sea. Remove any leaves from the cauliflower and slice it into 1/3-inch slices. Heat the tomato sauce in a large skillet on medium heat. (It's best to use a fairly thick sauce for this dish so that it sticks to the cauliflower.) Drop the cauliflower slices into the boiling water for 3 minutes. Using a spider or mesh strainer, remove the cauliflower and place it directly into the warm sauce. Carefully toss to coat. Divide the tomato-sauce-coated cauliflower between two plates and sprinkle the pine nuts on top. Garnish with parsley, Parmesan, salt, and pepper.

THAI-INSPIRED GREEN CURRY WITH EGGPLANT AND PEPPERS

Our favorite gardener, TV host, and author P. Allen Smith issued us a challenge at the beginning of one recent summer: grow a collection of vegetables and herbs in one pot, and at harvest time, use it all to make one cohesive dish. We came to refer to it as the Patio to Plate Challenge. It was so fun to start from the most elemental point and see it all the way through for, you know, that certain type of heady and pride-filled locavore experience.

We love green curry, so for the challenge, we wanted to create our own version that was flavorful and delicious. As a bonus, this dish is fast, gluten-free, and vegan. Feel free to add a fried egg or crispy tofu if you'd like, but it's also great as is.

Serves 2-4.

- 2 CUPS FRESH BASIL LEAVES (MORE FOR GARNISH)
- 2 PORTIONS OF RICE NOODLES (FOR SERVING)
- 1 SPRIG OREGANO (STEM DISCARDED)
- 1-INCH PIECE FRESH GINGER
- 1 CLOVE GARLIC
- 1 TEASPOON SAMBAL
- 1 LIME

- 1 13.5-OUNCE CAN COCONUT MILK
- 1 TEASPOON CHAMPAGNE OR RICE VINEGAR
- 2 CUPS SLICED JAPANESE EGGPLANT (1/4-INCH SLICES)
- 2 CUPS SLICED GREEN BELL PEPPERS (1/4-INCH SLICES)
- 1/2 CUP SLICED GREEN ONION (WHITE AND GREEN PARTS)

- 1 TEASPOON CORIANDER
- 1 TEASPOON CUMIN
- 1 TEASPOON TURMERIC
- KOSHER SALT AND CRACKED BLACK PEPPER (TO TASTE)
- 1 TABLESPOON OLIVE OIL (OR COCONUT OIL)

The secret to the bright green curry sauce is blanching the basil. Don't skip this step or you'll have a black sauce. Get a large pot of salted water up to a boil. You'll use this both to blanch the basil and to cook the rice noodles. With a bowl of ice water at the ready, drop the basil into the boiling, salted water and wait for it to turn bright green—this only takes a few seconds. Using a spider or a mesh strainer, scoop the basil out and drop it into the ice water. Once it's cooled, collect the basil and squeeze it dry.

Cook the noodles according to package directions. Drizzle the drained noodles with olive or coconut oil to prevent sticking, cover, and set aside until ready to serve.

Make the green curry sauce by blending the blanched basil, oregano, ginger, garlic, sambal, the zest of the lime, coconut milk, and vinegar together until smooth. Set aside.

In a large bowl, mix together the sliced eggplant, peppers, and onion with the coriander, cumin, and turmeric. Add salt and pepper to taste.

Next, get a wok or large sauté pan smoking hot. Add the oil and allow it to smoke. Once it starts smoking, carefully add the vegetable mixture and be sure to toss it every minute to allow it to brown evenly. Add the green curry sauce and allow it to heat through. Divide noodles into 2 to 4 bowls. To serve, spoon curry over noodles and garnish with a few basil leaves and lime wedges.

CAULIFLOWER CHOPS

- 2 LARGE HEADS CAULIFLOWER
- 1 TABLESPOON OLIVE OIL
- 1 TEASPOON SHERRY VINEGAR
- 1 TEASPOON BALSAMIC VINEGAR
- KOSHER SALT AND CRACKED
  BLACK PEPPER (TO TASTE)

Carefully trim the leaves away from the stem of each cauliflower but leave the stem intact. Quarter each cauliflower starting at the stem so you're left with 4 wedges from each for a total of 8. Place them on a parchment-lined baking sheet.

In a small bowl, combine the olive oil and sherry and balsamic vinegars. Brush each cauliflower liberally with the mixture. Place the cauliflower into a cold oven and set the temperature to 425 degrees. Bake for 45 to 50 minutes or until tender; be sure to flip the cauliflower halfway through the cooking time.

OLIVE-BAR PUTTANESCA WITH CAULIFLOWER CHOPS

We're so into this sauce. It's comprised of all the amazing things found on the olive bar and is made in the style of a spicy puttanesca sauce. First, grab a quart container at the olive bar and fill it up. We prefer a mix of spicy Kalamata and large green Greek olives. Next, throw in a bunch of sweet pickled peppers to add balance to your sauce. Lastly, top it off with a dozen or so of the roasted garlic cloves that are usually on the olive bar. You should have about a half quart of olives and about a half quart of peppers and garlic.

This puttanesca sauce is chunky and textured. We serve it over Cauliflower Chops, which are just big hunks of cauliflower roasted in the oven. The stem sticks out like a bone-in pork chop, so visually, it's pretty cool. The sauce is very flavorful, so leave it as is or top it with grated Romano cheese and pine nuts if you like.

Serves 4.

- CAULIFLOWER CHOPS (RECIPE ON PREVIOUS PAGE)
- 2 MEDIUM CARROTS
- 2 MEDIUM RIBS OF CELERY
- 2 MEDIUM SHALLOTS
- 1 QUART MIX OF SPICY OLIVES, SWEET PEPPERS, AND ROASTED GARLIC
- 1 TABLESPOON OLIVE OIL
- 1/2 CUP WHITE WINE (LIKE PINOT GRIGIO)
- 1 TEASPOON SALT-PACKED CAPERS (RINSED)
- 1 TEASPOON ITALIAN SEASONING
- 1 28-OUNCE CAN FIRE-ROASTED DICED TOMATOES
- GRATED ROMANO CHEESE AND TOASTED PINE NUTS (OPTIONAL, FOR GARNISH)

Using the slicing blade on the food processor, slice the carrots, celery, and shallots and set aside. Next, using the same blade, slice all of the stuff from the olive bar: pitted olives, sweet peppers, roasted garlic. Set the mixture aside in a separate bowl.

In a large skillet over medium heat, add the olive oil. Once the oil starts to shimmer, add the carrot, celery, and shallot mixture. Cook until softened and starting to brown, about 10 minutes. Add the wine and cook until most of the wine has evaporated. Add the sliced olive bar mixture along with the capers, Italian seasoning, and the tomatoes. Cook, uncovered, until everything is warmed through. There is no need to salt this sauce due to the salt content of the olives and capers. Serve the Cauliflower Chops family-style on a large platter and top with Olive-Bar Puttanesca. Garnish with Romano cheese and pine nuts.

SIMON MAJUMDAR'S LIFE-SAVING DAHL

Food Network host and author Simon Majumdar and I first met in Las Vegas outside the kitchen arena that was set up as the battleground for The World Food Championships. My buddy Ben Vaughn introduced us, and I handed Simon a copy of our first cookbook, *The Southern Vegetarian*. We immediately started talking about food. He told me that since his family is from India, vegetarian meals were common. Life-Saving Dahl, he told me, was always his favorite. He was kind enough to share his beloved dahl recipe!

Serves 4.

- 2-INCH PIECE FRESH GINGER
- 4 CLOVES GARLIC
- 3 FRESH GREEN CHILI PEPPERS (OR TO TASTE)
- 2 TABLESPOONS OLIVE OIL
- 2 CARDAMOM PODS
- 2 CLOVES
- 1 CINNAMON STICK
- 1 WHITE ONION (SLICED)
- 1 TEASPOON GROUND TURMERIC
- 1 TEASPOON POWDERED GINGER
- 1 TEASPOON CUMIN
- 1 TEASPOON CORIANDER SEED
- 1 TEASPOON HOT CHILI POWDER (OR TO TASTE)
- 1 TEASPOON SUGAR
- 1/2 TEASPOON KOSHER SALT
- 1 CUP OF RED LENTILS (I TOAST THESE FIRST IN A DRY PAN, USING MY FINGERS TO STIR, AND WHEN IT IS TOO HOT TO TOUCH, IT IS DONE. THIS GIVES A NUTTY FLAVOR TO THE LENTILS.)
- 3 CUPS WATER OR VEGETABLE STOCK
- 1 LEMON (CHOPPED INTO EIGHTHS)
- 1 9-OUNCE BAG OF SPINACH
- 4 HARD-BOILED EGGS

In the work bowl of your food processor, make a paste by blending the ginger and garlic with a little salt and water. Finely mince the fresh chili peppers. Put 2 tablespoons of oil into a hot pan, and when it comes to heat, add the cardamom, cloves, and cinnamon stick. Cook for 1 minute on a low heat. Add the onion and cook on a low heat until it begins to soften and turn golden. Don't rush this as you want the natural sweetness of the onions to be released. Add the ginger and garlic paste and cook for 2 to 4 minutes until it loses its raw quality. Add the minced chilies and cook for four minutes. Add the ground spices, sugar, and salt and mix well with the onions. Cook for 4 minutes until the spices lose their rawness. If the mixture begins to stick, add a little water. Add the lentils and mix well so they're all covered with the mixture. Add 3 cups of water or stock and the lemon pieces.

Simmer for 30 minutes until the lentils have broken down. (Add more water if it sticks to the pan.) If you like the dahl to be more chunky, leave as it is, but I sometimes whisk it gently to break the lentils down even further. Add the spinach, cover and allow to wilt into the lentils. The end result is great served over a hard-boiled egg.

SPAGHETTI SQUASH RIBS

This is reminiscent of the ubiquitous BBQ jackfruit recipes out there on the internet, but it uses a readily available fresh product instead of a canned one. The texture is perfect! In addition, the hot grill adds that indescribable smoky awesomeness that BBQ needs. Give this a shot—we think everyone will be amused by the presentation, and in addition, will also love it.

Serves 2 as a main dish or 4 as an appetizer.

- 1 MEDIUM SPAGHETTI SQUASH
- 1 TABLESPOON OLIVE OIL
- 1 TEASPOON SESAME OIL

- 1 TABLESPOON OF THE CHUBBY VEGETARIAN'S SIGNATURE MEMPHIS DRY RUB (PAGE 252)

- 1 CUP BBQ SAUCE (WARMED)

Preheat your outdoor grill to high. Using a serrated peeler or a sharp knife and plenty of caution, peel the squash. Cut the squash lengthwise and scoop out the seeds. Cut into 1/2-inch slices and discard the ends. On a large sheet pan, toss the sliced squash with the olive and sesame oil and then the dry rub until it's well-coated.

Grill the slices of squash for 4 to 5 minutes per side or until cooked through and well-marked by the grill. Arrange the slices of squash on a plate and brush with BBQ sauce. Serve more sauce on the side for dipping along with some Purple Cabbage Slaw (page 88).

For the 'Pulled' version, allow the cooked squash to cool. Pull or cut the skin away. Roughly chop the squash into about 1-inch pieces. Toss with the BBQ sauce and pull some of the chopped pieces apart.

TACO SALAD WITH CUMIN-SPICED MUSHROOM MEAT

Back in the '90s, the components for this type of salad were iceberg lettuce, pre-shredded cheddar, a jar of salsa, some sliced black olives, sour cream, and ground beef. Today, we tend to incorporate more vegetables into dinnertime, and we bake our tortilla bowls rather than frying them. You're likely to find sliced avocado, sautéed poblano peppers, homemade salsa, cilantro leaves, and our cumin-spiced Mushroom Meat as a healthier alternative to the ground beef. The best part is that this recipe is infinitely customizable. Feel free to throw in some black beans, quinoa, queso fresco, Greek yogurt, or pickled jalapeños.

Serves 4.

- CUMIN-SPICED MUSHROOM MEAT (RECIPE FOLLOWS)
- 4 LARGE WHOLE WHEAT TORTILLAS
- 1 TABLESPOON OLIVE OIL
- HONEY-LIME VINAIGRETTE (RECIPE FOLLOWS)
- 6 CUPS CHOPPED ROMAINE
- 2 AVOCADOS (PEELED AND SLICED)
- 2 CUPS SHREDDED CHEDDAR CHEESE
- 1 1/2 CUPS SALSA
- CILANTRO LEAVES
- HOT SAUCE
- 2 SAUTÉED, SLICED POBLANO PEPPERS (TO GARNISH)

Preheat your oven to 350 degrees. Make the Cumin-Spiced Mushroom Meat according to the recipe and set aside. Brush the tortillas with the olive oil and drape them over medium-sized, heat-proof bowls. Place the bowls on a large baking sheet and bake in the oven for 10-15 minutes or until the shells are golden and crispy. Remove from the oven and allow to cool.

Make the Honey-Lime Vinaigrette according to the recipe. Toss the romaine with the dressing and assemble the salads. Divide the dressed romaine among the bowls and top with 3/4 cup mushroom meat. Garnish with avocado, cheese, salsa, cilantro, hot sauce, and poblano peppers.

HONEY-LIME VINAIGRETTE

- JUICE OF 2 LIMES (ABOUT 1/4 CUP)
- ZEST OF 1 LIME
- 2 TABLESPOONS HONEY
- 1/4 CUP OLIVE OIL
- 1/8 TEASPOON CAYENNE PEPPER
- KOSHER SALT AND CRACKED BLACK PEPPER (TO TASTE)

Place the lime juice, zest, honey, olive oil, cayenne pepper, salt, and pepper in a small jar with a lid and shake it until the dressing emulsifies. Set aside until ready to use. (Makes about 1/2 cup.)

CUMIN-SPICED MUSHROOM MEAT

- 3 CUPS ROUGHLY CHOPPED PORTOBELLO MUSHROOMS (ABOUT 3 MEDIUM)
- 3 CUPS ROUGHLY CHOPPED EGGPLANT (PEELED, ABOUT 1 MEDIUM)
- 2 CUPS ROUGHLY CHOPPED WHITE ONION (ABOUT 1 MEDIUM)
- 2 BOUILLON CUBES (VEGETARIAN)
- 1/4 CUP OLIVE OIL
- 2 TABLESPOONS BALSAMIC VINEGAR
- 1 TEASPOON GARLIC POWDER
- 1/8 TEASPOON CRACKED BLACK PEPPER
- 1 1/2 TEASPOONS CUMIN
- 1 TEASPOON ANCHO CHILI POWDER
- 1/2 TEASPOON CHIPOTLE PEPPER POWDER

Preheat your oven to 350 degrees. Add the chopped mushrooms, stems and all, to your food processor and pulse 3 times or until finely chopped—you don't want to turn the vegetables into a fine paste; the pieces should be about the size of a black-eyed pea. Place processed mushrooms onto a large, parchment-lined, 17 x 12-inch rimmed baking sheet. Pulse the roughly chopped eggplant in the food processor in the same manner. Place eggplant onto the sheet pan beside the mushrooms. Repeat this process with the onion.

Crumble the bouillon cubes into the pile of processed vegetables. Drizzle the mound of mushrooms, eggplant, and onion with the olive oil and vinegar. Using your hands, toss it all together. Spread the mixture evenly over the sheet pan. Sprinkle the mixture with garlic powder, pepper, cumin, ancho chili powder, and chipotle pepper powder. Bake it for a total of 20 minutes. Remove the mixture and allow it to cool in the pan. (Makes 4 cups.)

NOTE: Some eggplants will contain more water than others. If there is excess moisture in the bottom of the pan, drain it off using a colander. Reserve the liquid—it's very flavorful—to add to soups or stews.

NASHVILLE HOT CHICKEN-STYLE HEN OF THE WOODS MUSHROOMS

Purists, beware: this will not please you in the least. For one, it's not chicken, so there's that. For two, while we were inspired by the hot chicken Nashville made famous, we do not intend for this to be a replication, just a vegetarian tribute to the real deal. That said, it's pretty awesome!

The texture of the hen of the woods mushrooms—they're also known as maitake mushrooms—is perfect for this. Be aware that the spice, while not overwhelming, is still really hot! You can add more or less cayenne pepper as your taste dictates.

Serves 2.

- VEGETABLE OIL (FOR FRYING)
- 2 TABLESPOONS SMOKED PAPRIKA
- 1/2 TEASPOON CAYENNE PEPPER
- 1/2 TEASPOON CRACKED BLACK PEPPER
- 1 1/2 TEASPOON KOSHER SALT

- 1 TEASPOON GRANULATED GARLIC
- 1 TEASPOON SUGAR
- 1/4 CUP 2% GREEK YOGURT
- 1/2 CUP 2% MILK
- 1 LARGE EGG (BEATEN)

- 2 LARGE HEN OF THE WOODS MUSHROOMS (SLICED IN HALF)
- 1 CUP ALL-PURPOSE FLOUR
- 2 SLICES WHOLE WHEAT BREAD
- GARLIC DILL PICKLES (FOR GARNISH)

In a 4-quart saucepan over medium heat, add enough oil to fill halfway. You want the oil temperature to be 350 degrees. Prepare the rest of the recipe while the oil heats up. In a small bowl, mix together the paprika, cayenne pepper, black pepper, salt, garlic, and sugar and set aside. In a large bowl, whisk together the yogurt, milk, egg, and half of the spice mixture. Carefully toss the mushrooms in the yogurt and egg mixture and allow them to rest in the fridge for 10 to 15 minutes.

Using a food thermometer, check to make sure your oil is at 350 degrees. Add the remainder of the spices to a large food storage bag along with the flour. Shake to incorporate. Remove the mushrooms from the yogurt and egg mixture and add them to the bag. Carefully move the mushrooms around to coat with the flour mixture.

Shake off any excess flour. Carefully add the flour-coated mushrooms to the oil. Cook for 8 to 10 minutes or until golden and crispy. Drain on paper towels. Serve on bread garnished with pickles.

CAULIFLOWER STEAK WITH CONFIT MUSHROOM PILAF, HERBED TOMATOES, CHEDDAR-PARSLEY BUTTER, AND FRIED CAPERS

(82 QUEEN'S RECIPE, REVISED FOR THE HOME COOK)

We met Executive Corporate Chef Steven Lusby, Berkley Spivey, and the amazing crew of Charleston, South Carolina's 82 Queen while we were in NYC for our James Beard Foundation presentation. Fate had us all cooking in the same kitchen that day. We were making 3 different snacks for 25 people, and they were making an 8-course dinner for 65 folks. We were nervous, but can you imagine the pressure on those guys? Yet it didn't seem to wear on them at all. They were so gracious and amazing from the first second we met them.

We kind of knew we'd be all right when we discovered that they were all fellow Southerners. "We update Southern classics," Chef Lusby told us of their cooking style. "Us, too!" I exclaimed, "But with vegetables." It was a great morning in the kitchen with them. We'd all brought our revised and curated versions of Southern cuisine up North to showcase. Our event was great, and Chef Spivey reports that their dinner that night was amazing, and they can't wait to be invited back. (Same here!)

Later, we were checking out the menu at 82 Queen and came across this impressive vegetarian dish for cauliflower steak. They were kind enough to share the recipe with us so that we could share it with you.

Serves 2.

- 1 LARGE HEAD CAULIFLOWER
- 1 TABLESPOON OLIVE OIL
- KOSHER SALT AND CRACKED BLACK PEPPER (TO TASTE)
- 1 1/2 TABLESPOONS WHITE TRUFFLE OIL

- CONFIT MUSHROOM PILAF (RECIPE FOLLOWS)
- HERBED TOMATOES (RECIPE FOLLOWS)
- CHEDDAR-PARSLEY BUTTER (RECIPE FOLLOWS)

- FRIED CAPERS (RECIPE FOLLOWS)

Carefully remove all green leaves attached to the stem of the cauliflower. Slice the cauliflower from the bottom into two 1-inch steaks; make sure each steak has a connection with the stem to prevent crumbling. (Reserve the remaining cauliflower for the Confit Mushroom Pilaf in the accompanying recipe.) Season lightly with olive oil, salt, and pepper. Place each steak directly on a hot grill and cook for about 7 to 8 minutes on each side, creating thatch marks. The cauliflower should be cooked through but still al dente. Lightly drizzle truffle oil equally over each cauliflower steak.

Assemble the dish by placing 1 1/2 cups of the Confit Mushroom Pilaf in the center of a plate. Place a few of the Herbed Tomatoes off to the side. Top the pilaf with one Cauliflower Steak. Garnish the dish with a slice of Cheddar-Parsley Butter and Fried Capers.

NOTE: This dish can be made vegan by omitting the Cheddar-Parsley Butter.

CONFIT MUSHROOM PILAF

- 4 CUPS OF CRIMINI MUSHROOMS (CLEANED, QUARTERED)
- 8 CLOVES PEELED GARLIC
- 1 SPRIG ROSEMARY
- 2 SPRIGS THYME
- 1/2 CUP OLIVE OIL
- RESERVED CAULIFLOWER (THAT WAS CUT AWAY FROM THE STEAKS)
- 1 SMALL WHITE ONION (FINELY DICED)
- KOSHER SALT AND CRACKED BLACK PEPPER (TO TASTE)

Preheat your oven to 350 degrees. Place all the ingredients on a large, parchment-lined baking tray. (The mushrooms should have enough room to move around.) Cover with parchment and then with aluminum foil and bake for 30 minutes. Let it cool at room temperature. Discard garlic and herbs; reserve oil and mushrooms.

In the work bowl of your food processor, pulse the cauliflower until it's broken down into rice-sized bits. Set aside.

In a large frying pan over medium-high heat, add a tablespoon of the reserved oil and the onion. Once the onion is translucent, add the cauliflower and cook until just tender, about 5 minutes. Fold in the mushrooms. Season with salt and pepper to taste. Cover and keep warm on the stove until ready to serve.

CHEDDAR-PARSLEY BUTTER

- 2 TABLESPOONS UNSALTED BUTTER (GRATED ON A CHEESE GRATER)
- 1 CUP OF FINELY GRATED CHEDDAR CHEESE
- 1 TEASPOON VERY FINELY CHOPPED PARSLEY
- KOSHER SALT AND CRACKED BLACK PEPPER (TO TASTE)

Place the cold butter, cheddar, parsley, salt, and pepper into small bowl and knead it with your fingers until all ingredients are well-incorporated. Lay out a sheet of parchment paper and lay butter in a line about 4 inches from the bottom and sides. Fold the sides of the parchment over the butter and tightly roll from the bottom, creating a cylinder. Refrigerate until firm. Using a hot knife, slice the butter into ¼-inch rounds. Extra can be stored in your refrigerator for a few days or frozen. (Makes about 2/3 cup.)

FRIED CAPERS

- 1/4 CUP CAPERS
- 1/2 CUP OLIVE OIL

First, strain off any liquid from the capers. In a small frying pan over medium heat, heat the oil until it starts to shimmer. Add the capers and fry for 2 minutes or just until the skin starts to peel. Set aside on a paper towel until you're ready to use them as a garnish.

HERBED TOMATOES

- 8 ROMA TOMATOES, STEMMED AND HALVED
- 1 TABLESPOON MINCED GARLIC
- 1 TABLESPOON FINELY CHOPPED THYME
- 1 TABLESPOON FINELY CHOPPED ROSEMARY
- 1 TABLESPOON FINELY CHOPPED BASIL
- 1 TABLESPOON OLIVE OIL
- KOSHER SALT AND CRACKED BLACK PEPPER
  (TO TASTE)

In a large bowl, combine all ingredients and mix thoroughly. Lay out tomatoes seed-side-up and roast in the oven at 350 degrees for about 20 minutes, or until the skins are lightly blistered. Set aside until ready to assemble the dish. (Makes 16 tomato halves.)

COLD-OVEN SWEET POTATO FRIES

- 2 LARGE SWEET POTATOES
  (PEELED AND CUT INTO 1/4-INCH BATONS)
- 2 TEASPOONS OLIVE OIL
- KOSHER SALT AND CRACKED BLACK PEPPER
  (TO TASTE)

In a large bowl, toss the sweet potatoes with the olive oil, salt, and pepper. Spread the potatoes out in a single layer on a parchment-lined baking sheet. Place into a cold oven and set the temperature to 415 degrees. Check them in 15 minutes or so. They should be golden and ready in 20-25 minutes. (Makes 2 servings, so you'll need to make several batches if you're serving lots of people.)

MEATY PORTOBELLO CHILI WITH COLD-OVEN SWEET POTATO FRIES

We're definitely not loyal to the Paleo diet, but sometimes we love to cook with parameters. Whether we're making a dish for friends or family members who are on a special diet or we just want to see what the latest food craze requires us to use or to omit, we're always up for a new challenge. This portobello chili is our take on Paleo cuisine with the ubiquitous sweet potato in the co-starring role.

Serves 6.

- 1 TABLESPOON COCONUT OIL
- 2 CUPS ONION (ABOUT 2 MEDIUM)
- 2 TEASPOONS ANCHO CHILI POWDER
- 2 TEASPOONS SMOKED PAPRIKA
- 2 TEASPOONS GRANULATED GARLIC

- 2 TEASPOONS KOSHER SALT
- 2 TEASPOONS CRACKED BLACK PEPPER
- 1 TEASPOON CUMIN
- 1 1/2 CUPS DICED BELL PEPPERS (ABOUT 2 MEDIUM)
- 8 CUPS CUBED PORTOBELLO (ABOUT 6 MEDIUM)
- 1 28-OUNCE CAN FIRE-ROASTED CRUSHED TOMATOES

- 1 TABLESPOON DRIED, CRUMBLED PORCINI
- 1/2 CUP VEGETABLE BROTH
- 2 TABLESPOONS SHERRY VINEGAR
- COLD OVEN SWEET POTATO FRIES (RECIPE ON PREVIOUS PAGE)
- SLICED AVOCADO (TO GARNISH)

In a large soup pot or Dutch oven over medium heat, melt the coconut oil and add the onion. Take your time with this step. You want to cook the onion for 15 minutes or so, stirring occasionally until nice and brown. This is where much of the flavor originates. Add the ancho, paprika, garlic, salt, pepper, and cumin and cook for another 5 minutes or until a nice fond, the brown layer stuck to the bottom of the pot, has formed.

Add in the peppers, portobellos, tomatoes, crumbled porcini, broth, and vinegar. Using a wooden spoon, scrape up the fond from the bottom of the pot and stir it in. Bring pot to a low boil and then reduce to the lowest heat. Cover and cook for one hour.

Serve over Cold-Oven Sweet Potato Fries and garnish with sliced avocado and anything else you'd like.

BUTTERNUT SQUASH STEAK WITH CHEF KELLY ENGLISH'S CHIMICHURRI

Here we've seasoned the squash with Montreal Steak Seasoning, a bright, smoky, and slightly spicy seasoning blend that works really well for this dish. For extra depth of flavor, we add sliced sautéed mushrooms before finishing the dish with a hearty spoonful of Chef Kelly English's Chimichurri. We could eat this every day! It's hugely flavorful, healthy, and it's even vegan.

Serves 4.

- 1 LARGE BUTTERNUT SQUASH
- 2 TABLESPOONS OLIVE OIL (DIVIDED)
- MONTREAL STEAK SEASONING (RECIPE FOLLOWS)
- 8 OUNCES CRIMINI MUSHROOMS (SLICED)
- CHEF KELLY ENGLISH'S CHIMICHURRI (RECIPE FOLLOWS)
- 2 FRESNO PEPPERS (SLICED)

First, select a large butternut squash that has a fat neck and a small bulb. You will get larger cuts from a squash that has this shape. Trim the stem end off and peel the squash using a serrated peeler. Cut the bulb-end of the squash off and reserve it for another use. Cut the neck into 4 equal pieces that are about 3/4 of an inch thick.

Preheat your outdoor grill to high. Drizzle the cut squash with 1 tablespoon of olive oil to coat. Season with a generous amount of Montreal Steak Seasoning on both sides of the squash. Grill squash for 8 minutes per side or until it's well-marked by the grill grates and also tender.

In a frying pan over high heat, add the remaining tablespoon of olive oil, the mushrooms, and 1/2 teaspoon of the Montreal Steak Seasoning. Cook, stirring occasionally, until the mushrooms are browned. Assemble the dish by dividing the mushrooms among the squash steaks and topping them with a few spoonfuls of Chef Kelly English's Chimichurri and sliced Fresno peppers.

MONTREAL STEAK SEASONING

- 1 TEASPOON SMOKED PAPRIKA
- 1 TEASPOON SWEET PAPRIKA
- 1 TEASPOON GRANULATED GARLIC
- 1 TEASPOON DRIED DILL
- 1 TEASPOON GROUND CORIANDER
- 1 TEASPOON CRACKED BLACK PEPPER
- 1 TEASPOON KOSHER SALT
- CAYENNE PEPPER (TO TASTE)

In a small bowl, mix the spices. Set aside until ready to season the squash. Store the leftover mix in an airtight container for up to a year. (Makes about 1/8 cup.)

CHEF KELLY ENGLISH'S CHIMICHURRI

- ¼ CUP THINLY SLICED CILANTRO LEAVES
- ¼ CUP THINLY SLICED PARSLEY LEAVES
- ¼ CUP THINLY SLICED GREEN ONIONS
- JUICE OF 1 LIME
- 2 TABLESPOONS RED WINE VINEGAR
- ½ CUP OLIVE OIL
- 1 TEASPOON CUMIN
- KOSHER SALT AND CRACKED BLACK PEPPER (TO TASTE)

In a medium bowl, mix together the cilantro, parsley, green onion, lime juice, vinegar, olive oil, and cumin. Season mixture with salt and pepper. (Makes about 3/4 cup.)

MUSTARD VINAIGRETTE

- 2 TABLESPOONS OLIVE OIL
- 1 TABLESPOON HONEY
- 1 TABLESPOON CHAMPAGNE VINEGAR
- 1 TABLESPOON GRAINY MUSTARD
  (LIKE ZATARAIN'S®)
- KOSHER SALT AND CRACKED BLACK PEPPER
  (TO TASTE)

Place the olive oil, honey, vinegar, mustard, salt, and pepper into a 1/2-pint Mason jar, screw on the lid, and shake it until the dressing is emulsified. Set aside until ready to use. (Makes about 1/4 cup.)

CEDAR PLANK WILD MUSHROOMS WITH MUSTARD VINAIGRETTE

Vegetarians, go ahead and claim some cedar plank space on the grill! Using a few different kinds of wild mushrooms works out really well with this method—and as a bonus, it will fill the air with the amazing smell of cedar smoke.

This strikes us as the type of vegetarian main dish that could compete with the usual old-school proteins in terms of heartiness and flavor, and it would be a super-convincing Meatless Monday idea for anyone who may be reluctant to try something different. Really, who could resist having what looks like a mini-still life of a beautiful forest floor for dinner?

Serves 2.

- 1 16-INCH CEDAR PLANK (OR 2 8-INCH PLANKS)
- 4 TO 5 NEW POTATOES (QUARTERED)
- 3 TO 4 CUPS OF ASSORTED WILD MUSHROOMS (LIKE CHANTERELLE, HEN OF THE WOODS, OR LARGE MORELS)
- 1 ONION (PEELED AND CUT INTO HALF-MOONS)
- MUSTARD VINAIGRETTE (RECIPE ON PREVIOUS PAGE)
- 2 TO 3 OUNCES SOFT GOAT CHEESE
- FRESH DILL, PARSLEY, AND CHIVES (TO GARNISH)

Soak cedar plank in water for at least one hour. Blanch the potatoes in salted water until fork-tender but not falling apart. Set aside.

Preheat your outdoor grill to medium. (The temperature gauge should be between 350 and 425 degrees.)

In a large bowl, toss the clean mushrooms and sliced onions with the Mustard Vinaigrette. Place the empty cedar plank down onto the grill for 4 minutes to heat one side. Remove the plank from the grill and arrange the potatoes on the warmed, marked side of the plank. Top the potatoes with the onion slices and mushrooms. Return the plank to the grill, shut the lid, and allow it to cook for 10 minutes. Next, place the chunks of goat cheese around the plank and cook for another 5 minutes. Garnish with dill, parsley, and chives.

FRESH SPRING PEAS AND CARROT GNOCCHI WITH MINT PESTO

Remember cans of mixed peas and carrots? This is in homage to that can of craziness, but here, we freshened it up and got it ready for springtime with mint, Vidalia onions, and the season's first peas. It's a great dish to plan to make with all of that good stuff that's in abundance around Easter.

Serves 2-4.

- MINT PESTO (RECIPE FOLLOWS)
- 1 CUP DICED CARROT (2 MEDIUM CARROTS)
- 1 TABLESPOON WATER
- 1 EGG
- KOSHER SALT AND CRACKED BLACK PEPPER (TO TASTE)
- 1 CUP ALL-PURPOSE FLOUR
- 1 TABLESPOON UNSALTED BUTTER
- 3/4 CUP DICED VIDALIA ONION
- 1 CUP FRESH ENGLISH PEAS
- MANCHEGO CHEESE (TO GARNISH)

Make Mint Pesto according to the instructions. Set aside in the fridge until ready to assemble the dish. In a covered dish, microwave the carrots and water for 4 minutes. Allow the mixture to rest for an additional 4 minutes.

Place the cooked carrots and any remaining water into the work bowl of your food processor, add the egg, add a pinch of salt and pepper, and process until smooth. Add the flour and pulse until everything is incorporated. (It's important to process the mixture as little as possible once the flour is added so you don't end up with tough gnocchi.) Transfer the mixture to a one-gallon food storage bag and press it down into one corner of the bag.

Bring a large pot of salted water to a boil. In a large pan over medium heat, melt the butter and add the onions and peas. Cook, stirring occasionally, until the raw flavor has been drawn out of the onion and the peas are cooked through.

Cut the corner out of the plastic bag and hold bag over the boiling water. Squeeze the bag from the back and force the mixture out of the hole. Using kitchen shears, snip the dough every 1/4 inch or so and allow it to fall into the water. Once all the gnocchi have floated to the top, retrieve them using a spider or mesh strainer and add them to the pea and onion mixture.

To plate, spread 1/4 of the pesto into the center of a plate. Spoon the gnocchi, pea, and onion mixture over the pesto and garnish with Manchego.

NOTE: Special equipment: 1 one-gallon food storage bag

MINT PESTO

- 1/4 CUP PINE NUTS (TOASTED)
- 1 CUP LOOSELY PACKED MINT LEAVES
- ZEST OF 1 LEMON
- 1 CLOVE GARLIC
- 1/8 TEASPOON SUGAR
- KOSHER SALT AND CRACKED
  BLACK PEPPER (TO TASTE)
- 1/4 CUP OLIVE OIL

Into the work bowl of your food processor, place the pine nuts, mint leaves, lemon zest, garlic, sugar, salt, and pepper. Turn the processor on and drizzle in the olive oil to form a paste. Set aside. (Makes about 3/4 cup.)

QUICK ASIAN PICKLES

- 1 CUCUMBER (THINLY SLICED)
- 1/2 CUP RICE VINEGAR
- 1/2 CUP WATER
- 1 TEASPOON KOSHER SALT
- 1 TABLESPOON SUGAR

Place the cucumber slices into a pint jar. In a medium mixing bowl, whisk together the vinegar, water, salt, and sugar. Pour the pickling liquid over the cucumbers, place a lid on the jar, and refrigerate for at least an hour and up to a week. (Makes about 2 cups.)

ROASTED RED PEPPER KOREAN BBQ SAUCE

- 2 MEDIUM ROASTED RED PEPPERS (STEMMED, SEEDED)
- 1 TABLESPOON SUGAR
- 2 TABLESPOONS SOY SAUCE (LIKE BRAGG® LIQUID AMINOS)
- 1 TABLESPOON SAMBAL
- 1 TABLESPOON RICE VINEGAR
- 1 TEASPOON SESAME OIL
- 1/4 TEASPOON POWDERED GINGER
- 1/4 TEASPOON GRANULATED GARLIC
- WHITE (OR BLACK) CRACKED PEPPER (TO TASTE)

Place the roasted red pepper, sugar, soy sauce, sambal, rice vinegar, sesame oil, ginger, garlic, and pepper in a food processor and blend until smooth. Store in an airtight container in the fridge for up to a week. (Makes about 1 cup.)

VEGETARIAN KOREAN BBQ MUSHROOM STEAMED BUNS

The first hurdle in getting ready to make these little wonders is to find the buns. They're a staple at any well-stocked Asian grocery. You'll find them in the freezer section under names like 'Lotus Bun' or 'Bun for Peking Duck' or 'Steamed Cakes.' Just look for the ones that are plain, as in not filled with anything like sweet bean paste or pork.

You can also find Korean BBQ sauce at the Asian market, but we prefer to make our own to avoid fish sauce and corn syrup. However, if you find a good vegetarian version of Korean BBQ sauce, by all means, use it!

Serves 12.

- QUICK ASIAN PICKLES (RECIPE ON PREVIOUS PAGE)
- ROASTED RED PEPPER KOREAN BBQ SAUCE (RECIPE ON PREVIOUS PAGE)

- 10 TO 12 FROZEN STEAMED BUNS (THE KIND THAT ARE A FOLDED CIRCLE WITH A HINGE)
- 1 TEASPOON TOASTED SESAME OIL
- 2 TEASPOONS OLIVE OIL

- 4 CUPS (ABOUT A POUND) SLICED MUSHROOMS (CRIMINI, SHIITAKE)
- CHOPPED ROASTED PEANUTS, CHOPPED GREEN ONION, AND CILANTRO (TO GARNISH)

Do ahead: Make the Quick Asian Pickles and the Roasted Red Pepper Korean BBQ Sauce.

Steam the frozen buns in a parchment-lined bamboo steamer for 10-15 minutes or until each bun is soft and pliable. Keep them all in the bamboo steamer until ready to serve.

In a large pan over high heat, heat the sesame oil and the olive oil until they start to smoke. Add the mushrooms to the pan in a single layer. Allow them to cook undisturbed for 3 minutes or until nicely browned on one side. Toss them around the pan and cook for another minute or two

until mushrooms appear to be heated through. Add the Roasted Red Pepper Korean BBQ Sauce to the pan and toss to coat. Remove from heat and cover to keep warm until ready to serve.

To assemble, stuff each bun with about 1/4 cup of the mushroom mixture, a few slices of the Quick Asian Pickles, a sprinkling of the chopped roasted peanuts, a few sliced green onions, and some cilantro.

NOTE: Special equipment: bamboo steamer

PURPLE POTATO PIEROGI

If you've never had a pierogi, allow us to describe it to you: it's like a cheesy, potato-y, onion-y ravioli that's been seared in butter. These things are, in a word, heaven. Not all pierogi are made with potatoes—some are made with sauerkraut, and some with fruit. We both like the potato ones best.

Here, we've used purple sweet potatoes and purple onion to make for a colorful surprise inside the little dumplings. It also makes for a slightly sweet foil to the sour nature of the sauerkraut.

Serves 4.

- 1 1/2 CUPS PEELED, CHOPPED PURPLE POTATO (ABOUT 1 MEDIUM)
- 3 TABLESPOONS UNSALTED BUTTER (DIVIDED)
- 1 1/4 CUPS FINELY DICED PURPLE ONION (ABOUT 1 MEDIUM)
- 1/4 CUP WHITE WINE (LIKE PINOT GRIGIO)
- 1 CUP SHREDDED SHARP WHITE CHEDDAR
- KOSHER SALT AND CRACKED BLACK PEPPER (TO TASTE)
- PIEROGI DOUGH (RECIPE FOLLOWS)
- 1 CUP VEGETABLE BROTH
- SAUERKRAUT, SOUR CREAM, AND CHIVES TO GARNISH

Boil the potato in salted water until tender (about 8 minutes), drain, and set aside in a large bowl. In a medium frying pan over medium heat, melt 1 tablespoon of the butter and cook the onion until it's translucent and starting to brown. Deglaze the pan with the wine and cook until most of the liquid has evaporated. Add the onion to the potato and mash until no large pieces of potato are left; you want it to have texture. Fold in the shredded cheese and add salt and pepper to taste.

Roll the dough out on your pasta maker starting at a #1 setting and work your way to the #5 setting. (Alternately, roll the dough out using a rolling pin to get the dough as thin as possible.) Using a spoon or small ice-cream scoop, place 1 heaping tablespoon of the potato filling near the bottom on one half of the large pasta sheet. Leaving about a half inch between each, continue to place mounds of potato filling down the length of the pasta (see page 155 for an example photo). Continue until all of the dough and filling have been used. You may re-roll scraps of dough if you have more filling to use. Fold the side of the dough without filling longways over the filling. Gently press the pasta around the filling to force out any air bubbles. Cut pierogi into half-moon shapes using a fluted pasta wheel.

Bring a large pot of salted water to a boil, and in a separate 12-inch frying pan, melt 1 tablespoon of butter over low heat. Boil 12 of the pierogi for about 3 minutes, turn up the heat under the butter to high, and transfer the boiled pierogi to the buttered pan; allow them to cook undisturbed for 2 to 2 1/2 minutes for a nice sear. Add 1/2 a cup of the vegetable broth and flip the pierogi using a pair of tongs. Repeat this process with the remaining pierogi or freeze them for another day.

Serve the pierogi of a bed of warm sauerkraut garnished with a dollop of sour cream and a sprinkling of chives. Spoon the pan sauce created with the broth and butter around the plate.

PIEROGI DOUGH

- 1 1/2 CUPS ALL-PURPOSE FLOUR
- 1 LARGE EGG (BEATEN)
- 1/2 CUP 2% GREEK YOGURT (OR SOUR CREAM)

Into a large bowl, add the flour and make a well in the center. Add the egg and the yogurt. Mix until a smooth dough forms. Cover dough and set it aside until you're ready to roll it out.

MEXICAN PIZZA

This fast-food inspired meal is the perfect thing when assembling—there's no way something this simple can even be called cooking—an easy dinner. We made it for the first time one late Thanksgiving night when leftovers were actually scarce, and it became a tradition to have it then and also for dinner on many weeknights throughout the year.

Serves 2.

- 2 10-INCH WHOLE WHEAT TORTILLAS
- 1 TABLESPOON OLIVE OIL
- 1 15-OUNCE CAN VEGETARIAN REFRIED PINTO BEANS
- 1 CUP SHREDDED SMOKED MOZZARELLA
- 2 LARGE AVOCADOS
- JUICE OF 1/2 LIME
- KOSHER SALT AND CRACKED BLACK PEPPER (TO TASTE)
- 1/2 CUP FINELY SHREDDED CABBAGE
- 1/2 CUP CHOPPED TOMATO
- 1 TABLESPOON CHOPPED CHIVES
- 1/4 CUP SLICED PICKLED JALAPEÑOS
- HOT SAUCE (TO TASTE)

Preheat your oven to 350 degrees. Brush both sides of each tortilla with the olive oil. Place on a large baking sheet so tortillas don't overlap. Cook in the oven for 15 to 20 minutes or until crispy. Remove from the oven and allow tortillas to cool enough to be handled.

Spread about half of the refried pinto beans onto each of the crispy tortillas. Now, sprinkle the cheese on one of the bean-covered tortillas. Return the tortillas to the oven for another 10 minutes or until the cheese has melted and the beans are warmed through.

Make a simple guacamole by combining the flesh of the avocado and the lime juice in a medium bowl and mashing it with a fork until there are no large chunks left. Add salt and pepper to taste. Set aside until ready to use.

Stack the bean-covered tortilla onto the bean-and-cheese-covered tortilla. Top that with all of the simple guacamole, cabbage, tomato, chives, pickled jalapeños, and hot sauce. Chop it into quarters and serve.

BAKED LEMONGRASS TOFU WITH COCONUT JASMINE RICE

This dish gets its fragrant kick from a mixture of fresh herbs that you may already be growing in your garden. The lemongrass, which can be found at a health food store or Asian market, adds a floral note, while the garlic and soy sauce add depth.

Don't be deterred by the length of this recipe; it's really quite simple when you break it down. Make the spice mixture, toss it with the tofu, bake, sauté onions, add coconut milk, and it's done. It's healthier than the deep-fried stuff you get when you go out—and also, you know exactly what's in this.

Serves 2.

- 1 13.5-OUNCE CAN COCONUT MILK
- 1 CUP JASMINE RICE
- 2 STALKS OF LEMONGRASS
- 1/2-INCH PIECE FRESH GINGER
- 3 CLOVES GARLIC
- 1 TEASPOON SUGAR
- 1/4 CUP MINT LEAVES

- 1/4 CUP BASIL LEAVES
- ZEST FROM 1 LIME
- 1 TABLESPOON SAMBAL (OR SRIRACHA)
- 1/4 CUP VEGETABLE OIL
- 2 BLOCKS FIRM TOFU (CUT INTO BITE-SIZED CUBES, PATTED DRY)
- KOSHER SALT (A PINCH)

- 1 ONION (SLICED INTO HALF MOONS)
- 1 TABLESPOON SOY SAUCE (LIKE BRAGG® LIQUID AMINOS)
- 1 HEAD BUTTER LETTUCE (TORN)
- 1 CUCUMBER (THINLY SLICED)
- 1 LARGE TOMATO (SLICED)

Preheat your oven to 400 degrees. On the stovetop, bring one cup of the coconut milk and one cup of water to a boil in a medium pot. Add the jasmine rice and cover. Reduce heat to low to allow the rice to simmer. It will take about 20 minutes for the rice to cook through and absorb all of the liquid.

Now comes the fun part: smack the stalks of lemongrass on the countertop to soften them and then split them open. Pull out the pliable inside part and place it in a food processor. Discard the rest of the stalk. Add the ginger, garlic, sugar, mint, basil, zest, and sambal to the food processor and pulse. These ingredients should be very finely chopped.

In a large bowl, toss the lemongrass mixture together with the vegetable oil and tofu and throw in a pinch of salt. Using a slotted spoon, transfer the tofu to a parchment-lined baking sheet and arrange the cubes into a single layer. Reserve the lemongrass and oil mixture that's at the bottom of the bowl. Bake the tofu for 20-30 minutes or until the edges start to brown. Don't let the garlic burn—keep a close eye on it.

While that's cooking in the oven, sauté the onion in a large frying pan over medium heat using the reserved lemongrass and oil mixture. Once the onion is soft and translucent, remove pan from the heat. Add a tablespoon of soy sauce to the onions. Once the tofu is done, remove it from the oven and toss it into the pan with the onions along with the remaining coconut milk. Mix and heat through. Serve over butter lettuce with sliced cucumbers and tomatoes and coconut rice.

CREAMED ARUGULA

- 1 5-OUNCE CONTAINER OF
  PRE-WASHED ARUGULA
- 1 TABLESPOON OLIVE OIL
- 2 GARLIC CLOVES (THINLY SLICED)
- 1 EGG (BEATEN)
- 2 OUNCES GOAT CHEESE
- 2 TABLESPOONS WATER OR MILK
- KOSHER SALT AND CRACKED BLACK PEPPER
  (TO TASTE)

Bring a large pot of salted water to a boil. Blanch the arugula in the super-salty water for a few seconds. Rinse and squeeze out any excess water. In a medium skillet over medium heat, sauté the garlic in olive oil until toasted. Add the blanched arugula, egg, cheese, and water or milk. Mix vigorously until the egg has cooked through. Add salt and pepper to taste. Remove from the heat and set aside. (Makes about 1 cup.)

SOCCA WITH CREAMED ARUGULA AND ARTICHOKE AND PINE NUT RAGOUT

Socca is so fast and simple to make. It's healthy, it's packed with flavor, and it's as versatile as pasta. So what the heck is socca, anyway? It's a crepe or pancake made from garbanzo bean flour. It's found in Italy and France, where it's typically eaten plain as a snack. We just couldn't help but to dress ours up for dinner with two amazing, savory arugula and artichoke side dishes.

Serves 8.

- 1 CUP GARBANZO BEAN FLOUR
- 1 1/4 CUPS WATER
- 2 TABLESPOONS OLIVE OIL (MORE FOR COOKING)
- 1 TEASPOON CRACKED BLACK PEPPER
- 1/4 TEASPOON KOSHER SALT
- GRATED PARMESAN CHEESE (FOR GARNISH)

Mix the garbanzo bean flour, water, olive oil, pepper, and salt with a whisk so there are no lumps; batter should be thinner than pancake batter. Set the mixture aside for at least 10 minutes. Heat a cast-iron skillet on medium heat. Using a silicone pastry brush, coat the surface of the skillet with about a teaspoon of olive oil. Pour 1/4 cup of batter into the skillet and keep your eye on it. Once the surface appears dry, after about 2 minutes, use a metal spatula to flip the socca. Allow it to cook for another 2 minutes and set aside. Repeat until all batter has been used.

To assemble, spread the creamed arugula on one side of the socca. Fold the socca into quarters and place onto the plate. Top with ragout and grated Parmesan.

ARTICHOKE AND PINE NUT RAGOUT

- 3 TABLESPOONS OLIVE OIL
- 1 LARGE SHALLOT (DICED)
- 1 CUP WHITE WINE
- PINCH OF SUGAR
- PINCH OF KOSHER SALT
- PINCH OF RED PEPPER FLAKES
- 1 TABLESPOON TOMATO PASTE
- 1 TABLESPOON OLIVE PASTE (OPTIONAL)
- 10 BABY ARTICHOKE HEARTS (HALVED)
- 1 RED BELL PEPPER (PEELED, DICED)
- 1/2 CUP MIXED OLIVES (CHOPPED)
- 1 LARGE TOMATO (PEELED, DICED)
- 1/4 CUP PINE NUTS
- 10 CAPERS
- 1/4 CUP CHOPPED PARSLEY

In a large skillet over medium high heat, sauté the shallot in olive oil until translucent. Add the wine, sugar, and salt. Reduce the mixture until it's thick and syrupy. Add the remaining ingredients and cook until heated through. (For this ragout, you do not want the vegetables to break down as they would in a tomato sauce.) (Makes about 3 cups.)

VEGETARIAN EGGPLANT TAJINE

We call this dish a tajine as a tribute to the earthenware pot in which something like this would normally be cooked. It's best described as a pie plate with an earthenware cone designed to be used to slowly simmer ingredients. Since we use eggplant and not some tough cut of meat, a regular old skillet will do just fine for the business at hand.

Look for ras el hanout at your local gourmet specialty store. A Moroccan spice mixture, it provides a complex array of warm spices like cumin, coriander, clove, and cinnamon and produces an aromatic mix of interesting flavors. The simmered eggplant provides a wonderfully meaty texture.

Serves 4.

- 1 MEDIUM WHITE ONION (DICED)
- 1 VEGETARIAN BOUILLON CUBE
- 1 HEAPING TABLESPOON RAS EL HANOUT
- ZEST OF 1 LEMON
- KOSHER SALT AND CRACKED BLACK PEPPER (TO TASTE)

- 1/2 TEASPOON GRANULATED GARLIC
- 1 CUP WHITE WINE (LIKE PINOT GRIGIO)
- 1 15-OUNCE CAN CHICKPEAS (DRAINED)
- 4 CUPS LARGE DICED EGGPLANT (1 LARGE OR 4 MEDIUM JAPANESE, PEELED)

- 2 MEDIUM GREEN PEPPERS (DICED)
- 1 15-OUNCE CAN STEWED TOMATOES
- SRIRACHA HOT SAUCE (TO TASTE)
- 2 CUPS PREPARED COUSCOUS
- GREEK YOGURT, MINT, AND LEMON ZEST (OPTIONAL, TO GARNISH)

Preheat your oven to 350 degrees. In a large oven-proof skillet with high sides over high heat, sauté the onion, bouillon cube, ras el hanout, lemon zest, salt, pepper, and granulated garlic in a dry pan. Once the onion starts to caramelize (about 3 minutes), add the wine and deglaze the pan. Reduce the liquid by half, and add the chickpeas, eggplant, green peppers, stewed tomatoes, and Sriracha. Stir to incorporate. Place in the oven for 30 minutes. Serve over couscous. Garnish with Greek yogurt, mint, and lemon zest.

GOAT CHEESE FILLING

- 10.5 OUNCES GOAT CHEESE
- 1 HEAD ROASTED GARLIC (PEELED)
- 1 LARGE EGG
- 1/2 CUP PANKO BREAD CRUMBS
- 4 SPRIGS OF THYME
- 1/2 TEASPOON CHAMPAGNE VINEGAR
- KOSHER SALT AND CRACKED BLACK PEPPER
  (TO TASTE)

Into the work bowl of your food processor, place the cheese, garlic, egg, panko, thyme, and vinegar. Pulse until all ingredients are well-incorporated. Add salt and pepper to taste. Place into a covered container and store in the fridge until needed. Rinse the food processor in order to use it for the next step. (Makes about 1 1/2 cups.)

BEET AND GOAT CHEESE RAVIOLI WITH PARSLEY AND MINT PESTO

This is a dish we make for company on special occasions. The bright and earthy pasta contrasts with the vibrant, green pesto—both on the plate and on the palate. It's a dish that screams '*Spring!*' by making use of the fresh herbs, eggs, and beets that start to appear at the market in April.

We don't write much about filled pastas like ravioli because they're pretty time-consuming to make, and also because we're self-aware enough to know we may have a reputation for not always having the simplest recipes in the world. (A common observation from some readers we meet: "So, y'all don't have any kids, right?") We'd hate to further bolster that notion about our sometimes-complicated-but-hopefully-worth-it food by asking you to make not only the filling of this ravioli from scratch, but also the pasta and, well, the pesto sauce that accompanies it…but, hey, here we go. Just humor us and come along and see what you think.

To be honest, we find this process relaxing, and possibly you will, too—just maybe not the very first time you make ravioli. It takes a few good tries before things really start to come together, but you do learn more with each go at it. It's best to think about ravioli-making as several little steps rather than one giant leap. Make the filling, make the pasta, fill the pasta, make the sauce, and serve. See, it's simple!

You will need some special equipment. We often use the food processor in our kitchen. If you don't already have one, get one! You'll also need a pasta roller. We have one that attaches to our stand mixer. It's much easier than a hand-crank, but one of those will do just fine. Lastly, you'll need a fluted pastry wheel. This is the thing that you'll use to cut the pasta. The fluted shape helps to seal the ravioli so they don't unravel in the water as they cook.

Let's go ahead and get started, but before we begin, place a head of garlic and 4 medium beets in a covered casserole dish and drizzle these ingredients with olive oil. Place into a 350-degree oven for about 1 to 1 1/2 hours or until the beets are cooked through. Allow everything to cool. You'll need these ingredients later on in the process. If you don't have the patience for that, just pick up a can of beets and also some roasted garlic from the olive bar at the grocery.

continued on next page →

Serves 6-8.

BEET PASTA

- 2 1/2 CUPS ALL-PURPOSE FLOUR
- 3/4 CUP PEELED, CHOPPED, ROASTED BEET (ABOUT 1 MEDIUM)
- 1 LARGE EGG
- ABOUT 3 TABLESPOONS WATER

Into the work bowl of your food processor, place the flour and beets. Let the food processor run until the roasted beet is completely blended into the flour. (The result will look like magenta sand.) Add the egg and blend. With the food processor running, add the water one tablespoon at a time until the dough forms a ball and runs around the container all clumped together; you'll see it when this happens. Gather the ball, wrap it in plastic wrap, and place it into the fridge to rest. Rinse the food processor in order to use it for the next step.

PESTO

- 1 LARGE BUNCH FRESH PARSLEY (LONG STEMS REMOVED, ABOUT 2 CUPS)
- 1 BUNCH FRESH MINT (ABOUT 1 CUP)
- 1 CLOVE GARLIC
- 1 CUP TOASTED HAZELNUTS (SKINS RUBBED OFF)
- JUICE OF 1 LEMON
- 1/2 CUP OLIVE OIL
- KOSHER SALT AND CRACKED BLACK PEPPER (TO TASTE)

Into the work bowl of your food processor, place the parsley, mint, garlic, hazelnuts, lemon juice, and olive oil. Pulse until everything is broken down but still chunky. Add salt and pepper to taste. Set aside until ready to assemble the dish. (Makes about 1 1/2 cups.)

To assemble the ravioli: Roll the pasta out starting at a #1 and working your way to a #5 on your pasta roller. (Cut pasta to fit your well-floured work surface if it gets too long.) You should end up with about four 3-foot sections of pasta dough. Using a small ice cream scoop or a spoon, place about a teaspoon of filling on one half of the large pasta sheet. Leaving about the width of two fingers between each, continue to do this down the length of the pasta. Fold the side that's without filling longways over the filling and press the pasta all around the filling using the sides of your hands. Using the fluted pastry wheel, cut the front edge off of the pasta and run it in between each lump of filling. The hinged side should be left as is. This will make about 30 large ravioli.

In batches of 10, drop the ravioli into a pot of well-salted water for about 2 minutes. Using a strainer, retrieve them from the water and toss in a large bowl with a teaspoon of olive oil to keep them from sticking together. Serve on a large platter garnished with the remaining beets and the pesto.

NOTE: Special equipment: stand mixer, pasta roller attachment, fluted pastry wheel

GINGER AND CASHEW STIR-FRY

I still remember how the shiny, enameled red lid of the electric wok would catch my eye as I sat on the kitchen counter and talked to my mom as she cooked. Those of us who lived through it can definitely recall the wok craze of the '70s and '80s. Everybody had one; our family was no exception. The three young vegetarians in the house grew up on soggy, salty stir-fry, and I carried this questionable tradition into my young adulthood. As a thrifty college student trying to start my own photography business, I'd budget $20 a week for groceries: fresh vegetables, rice, plus tempeh, eggs, or nuts for protein. So, what was (always) for dinner? Stir-fry! Sometimes I had it over rice and sometimes over noodles, but if we weren't having spaghetti, we were having stir-fry…admittedly, a pretty soggy stir-fry.

My version was so bad that my girlfriend, who's now my wife Amy, secretly hated it but covered by saying that she just wasn't in the mood for stir-fry. I think she hoped that I wouldn't catch on. What I didn't realize at the time is that my version of stir-fry lacked that signature wok flavor that comes from the ancient cooking vessel when it's in the hands of a true professional. So, I always started with a great assortment of fresh vegetables. That's good! What was I doing wrong? I was missing that crisp vegetable snap with plenty of intense flavor from the Malliard Reaction that happens when the vegetables brown from contact with the hot pan. And, for goodness sake, why was my stir-fry soggy? The answer, it turns out, is simple.

I recently asked James Beard Award-winning cookbook author and stir-fry guru Grace Young what's the single most important thing one needs in order to make a successful stir-fry meal at home. She told me, "I would say it starts with choosing the right pan. There are many people using nonstick woks or skillets, and that is guaranteed to produce a soggy, lackluster stir-fry." I could see myself in her words; I'm truly the Goldilocks of woks. I've had the plug-in electric kind, which didn't get any hotter than warm. I've had the round-bottomed kind with a wok ring for a conventional stovetop. I've had the nonstick variety, a true waste of money. I'll tell you from firsthand experience: don't buy any of these. Grace says, "I recommend a 14-inch flat-bottomed carbon-steel wok. It costs less than $25, and it will last you more than a lifetime." I agree—the 14-inch flat-bottom wok we've had for three years now has been the best option, for sure. It'll work on a gas or electric stove, and it offers the stability and control we all need in order to stir-fry correctly.

Season your new purchase (or your old wok if you've never seasoned it before) by following these simple steps. First, wash the new wok with liquid detergent and dry it thoroughly. Next, rub the inside of the wok with canola oil (or any oil with a high smoke point) and set it over a high flame until the whole pan darkens; this will take about six to eight minutes, depending on how hot the flame is. I recommend that you do this outside on your outdoor grill's side burner since it makes lots of smoke! Repeat the process after simply rinsing the cooled wok with water and drying it. This will ensure a good, slick coat. What is really happening when you season your wok is a chain reaction of chemical changes. It'll make your wok slippery where it needs to be, easier to use, and it won't rust. You want that! The result is that your brand-new wok will look ancient but work quite well...and that's the whole point.

Now let's head to the market. The wok makes it simple to eat seasonally, so pick up a few things that are at their best. Aim to stock your basket with a variety of colors and textures from the produce section. Choose hearty greens like kale, cruciferous vegetables like broccoli, an abundance of mushrooms like shiitake, fresh carrots, and because this is a stir-fry, we can't forget traditional Chinese vegetables such as bok choy. Add garlic, fresh ginger, and spring onions. We usually throw in a few sweet bell peppers for color.

The next step is to wash everything and thoroughly dry it. Shake off the excess water in the sink and then air-dry vegetables on a dishtowel to ensure that they're completely dry. This not only helps them last longer in storage, but we've found it to be crucial to the stir-frying process. Next, cut everything up into same-sized pieces so they cook quickly and evenly. No need to be too fussy about this—just eyeball it. Make sure to cut denser vegetables like carrots or the stem of the broccoli thin; a mandoline is a great tool for this, but you could just use a chef's knife. Toss the vegetables together and store them in a large lidded container in the fridge until you're ready to use them.

I also paid a visit to Wally Joe, Chef, Partner, and General Manager at Acre Restaurant in East Memphis. He was born in Hong Kong and raised in Cleveland, Mississippi, where his family's restaurant KC's had a real-deal wok station. "Don't be afraid of the wok," he told me after I'd let him in on my years of failure with it. "It's just like any other pan, but it's just a different shape." He laughed, "I break it out at home mostly to make a simple and easy noodle dish, stir-fry, or a curry." While it's just a pan of a different shape, I figured that there has to be a trick to it, so I asked for a hint. "Just remember to use high heat," he advised. "That's the best way to get the brown and crispy edges on the vegetables and noodles that are the hallmark of wok cooking."

"The wok is an easy pan to work with, but until recently, there hasn't been enough information to guide novice cooks," Grace reassured me. After years of learning what not to do, and after my conversations with Wally and Grace, I feel like I have a pretty good handle on it now. There's nothing left to it but to do it, so here's my new way with the wok.

The first thing to remember is to have everything ready to go: vegetables cut, sauce made, and rice or noodles prepared and set aside. It moves way faster than you'd think, though nowhere near as fast as a professional chef cooking over a real 200,000-BTU wok station. Put your seasoned wok over the highest heat on the stovetop and let it heat up until you see little wisps of smoke rise up off of the hot metal. Pour in the oil and wait for it to start to smoke, which is very important! If you put vegetables (or really anything) in a cold wok with cold oil, you simply won't get the results you desire—and your significant other will only eat it to be nice. Now, put your vegetable mixture into the wok and give a little shake. Never cook more than 4 cups of anything total in a wok; overcrowding the pan will result in the dreaded soggy stir-fry. Let the mixture rest in the hot pan for 45 seconds before tossing everything to redistribute it by pushing the pan forward and then jerking it back just like you'd do to flip an omelette or by using a spatula (maybe even stir-fry spatula!). You'll notice the browned edges of the vegetables that were touching the hottest part of the pan. That's flavor! Allow the vegetables to rest for another 45 seconds to 1 minute before flipping them again. Flip the vegetables one last time and allow them to cook for 1 minute. At this point, add your sauce and cook for one more minute. Once you notice the sauce starting to thicken, remove the stir-fry from the wok and place it in a serving bowl.

There is so much more to wok cooking, such as learning about the Bao and Chao techniques, but this primer will set you on the right path. I really appreciated that Grace shared this last bit of wisdom with me: "When you cook with a wok, you become a part of a cooking tradition that is over 2,000 years old. It's true that it takes a little time to learn how to work with it and care for it, but unlike most cookware, you'll develop a relationship with your wok. It is a pan to cherish."

Let's do a quick review of our simple stir-fry method: the right wok that's seasoned correctly, seasonal vegetables that are dry and cut to a uniform size, hot wok with hot oil, and slow it down just a little to attain that coveted wok flavor that comes from the browned edges of the vegetables. Avoid all the pitfalls I've experienced in the past by following these few simple steps! You, too, can have a beautiful, quick, and delicious meal of seasonal vegetables. Oh, and now after twenty years of avoiding my soggy stir-fry at all costs, my wife requests my new-and-improved, seasonal stir-fry on a weekly basis. That, my friends, is a victory.

Serves 2.

- 2 CUPS PREPARED RICE
- 4 CUPS SPRING VEGETABLE MIX (RECIPE FOLLOWS)
- 1/2 CUP VEGETABLE BROTH
- 2 TABLESPOONS SOY SAUCE (LIKE BRAGG® LIQUID AMINOS)

- 1 TABLESPOON SESAME OIL
- 1 TEASPOON SAMBAL (MORE TO TASTE)
- 1 TEASPOON RICE VINEGAR
- 3 CLOVES GARLIC (MINCED)
- 1-INCH PIECE FRESH GINGER (MINCED)

- 1 TEASPOON CORNSTARCH
- 1 TABLESPOON VEGETABLE OIL
- 1 SPRING ONION (SLICED)
- 1/2 CUP ROASTED AND SALTED CASHEWS

Prepare the rice according to package instructions. Prepare Spring Vegetable mix according to the recipe. In a pint-sized jar with a lid, add the broth, soy sauce, sesame oil, sambal, rice vinegar, garlic, ginger, and cornstarch. Screw on the lid and shake vigorously. Set sauce aside until ready to use.

Put your seasoned wok over the highest heat on the stovetop and let it heat up until you see little wisps of smoke rise up off of the hot metal. Pour in the vegetable oil and wait for it to start to smoke, which is very important! Now, carefully put your vegetable mixture into the wok and give a little shake. Let the mixture rest in the hot pan for 45 seconds before tossing everything to redistribute it by pushing the pan forward and then jerking it back just like you'd do to flip an omelette or by using a spatula. Allow the vegetables to rest for another 45 seconds to 1 minute before flipping them again. Flip the vegetables one last time and allow them to cook for 1 minute. At this point, add your sauce and cook for one more minute. Once you notice the sauce starting to thicken, remove the stir-fry from the wok and place it in a serving bowl. The whole cooking process takes about 4 minutes. Serve over rice and garnish with spring onions and cashews.

SPRING VEGETABLE MIX

- 2 CROWNS BROCCOLI
- 1 POUND SHIITAKE MUSHROOMS
- 2 SMALL OR 1 LARGE BOK CHOY
- 1 BUNCH LACINATO (DINOSAUR) KALE
- 2 LARGE OR 4 SMALL CARROTS
- 2 CUPS SNOW PEAS

Wash and dry everything thoroughly. Cut everything up into 1/8-inch to 1/4-inch slices. Store in an airtight container in the fridge.

MASALA DOSA

Years ago, we fell in love with dosas. We loved them so much that we wanted to learn how to make them in our own home. With a little guidance from our friend Krishna R. Chattu at Mayuri Indian Restaurant in Memphis, we got there. Now, being able to to make a successful batch of dosas feels wonderful. This was definitely a group effort with a lot of advice along the way!

Serves 6.

- 1 1/2 CUPS IDLY (OR IDLI) RICE
- 1/2 CUP URAD DAL (SMALL WHITE LENTILS)
- 1/4 TSP FENUGREEK (OR METHI) SEEDS
- KOSHER SALT (TO TASTE)
- DOSA FILLING (RECIPE FOLLOWS)
- SIMPLE SAMBAR (RECIPE FOLLOWS)

Into a medium bowl, place the rice, dal, and fenugreek seeds. Add 2 cups of water and stir. Cover bowl with a plate and leave covered mixture out on the counter overnight to begin to ferment.

The next day, process all the ingredients (including the water) in a blender for at least five minutes. Place the blended mixture in a large bowl and cover with plastic wrap. Allow the mixture to sit overnight in a warm place to continue the fermentation process. (The mixture will rise a little like a bread dough; that's how you know it has correctly fermented.) At this point, add salt to taste. Place the dosa batter in the refrigerator to chill since using a cold, very smooth, well-fermented dosa batter is key.

In a large cast-iron skillet or crepe pan over medium heat, cook the dosas one at a time. Use a metal ladle, pour about 1/2 cup in the center of the cast iron pan like you're making a pancake, and then push the batter outward in concentric circles. Keep your eye on the edges and the thinnest parts of the dosa. Once it starts to turn a deep brown, the dosa is ready to be removed from the pan. Use a butter knife or offset spatula to loosen the edges of the dosa, and then, using your fingers, peel the dosa from the skillet. Wipe the cast-iron pan clean with a towel in-between cooking each dosa.

If you're making dosas for more than a few people, it's perfectly fine to make them ahead of time. Stack them when they're cooked and store them in the fridge. They reheat nicely in a dry skillet.

When you're ready to serve your dosa, stuff it with about 1/2 cup of the dosa filling and fold it like a burrito. Add a side of Simple Sambar. No utensils needed. Just break off a piece, dunk it in sambar, and eat it with your hands.

SIMPLE SAMBAR

- 2 CUPS VEGETABLE STOCK
- 1/2 TEASPOON BLACK MUSTARD SEED
- 5 GREEN CARDAMOM PODS
- 1 TABLESPOON DRIED CURRY LEAVES
- 2 CLOVES GARLIC (SMASHED)
- 1 MEDIUM CELERY RIB (SLICED)
- 1 MEDIUM CARROT (SLICED)

In a medium pot, bring the stock, mustard seed, cardamom, curry leaves, garlic, celery, and carrot to a boil. Reduce to a simmer, cover, and simmer for 20 to 30 minutes. (Makes about 3 cups.)

DOSA FILLING

- 1 TABLESPOON UNSALTED BUTTER
- 1 TEASPOON TANDOORI MASALA
- 1 TEASPOON DRIED CURRY LEAVES
- 1/2 TEASPOON GROUND GINGER
- 1 MEDIUM WHITE ONION (THINLY SLICED INTO HALF-MOONS)
- 1 MEDIUM JALAPEÑO PEPPER (THINLY SLICED)
- 4 SMALL YUKON GOLD POTATOES (PEELED AND DICED, ABOUT 4 CUPS)
- JUICE OF 1 LIME
- 3/4 CUP FROZEN GREEN PEAS
- 1/2 TEASPOON KOSHER SALT

In a large skillet over medium-high heat, melt the butter. Add the masala, curry leaves, and ginger and cook for 2 minutes in order to toast the spices. Add the onion, jalapeño, potatoes, and lime juice, and stir to incorporate the ingredients. Reduce heat to medium. Cover and cook, stirring often, for 15 minutes or until the potatoes are tender. Add the peas and salt and lightly break up the potatoes with a fork. Set aside until ready to serve. (Makes 4 cups.)

SOFRITO

- 1 MEDIUM ROMA TOMATO
- 1 CUP LOOSE-PACKED FLAT-LEAF PARSLEY
- 1 MEDIUM YELLOW PEPPER (STEM AND SEEDS DISCARDED)
- 1 TABLESPOON SMOKED PAPRIKA
- 1 TABLESPOON SHERRY VINEGAR
- 1 MEDIUM SHALLOT
- 3 CLOVES GARLIC
- 1 TABLESPOON TOMATO PASTE

- 1/2 TEASPOON KOSHER SALT
- 1/2 TEASPOON CRACKED BLACK PEPPER

Into the work bowl of your food processor, place the tomato, parsley, yellow pepper, paprika, vinegar, shallot, garlic, tomato paste, salt, and pepper. Blend until everything is liquified. The mixture won't be completely smooth. Set aside in the fridge until ready to use. (Makes 1 1/2 cups.)

VEGETARIAN PAELLA

We'd like to share our process of making a paella without meat or seafood. It's kind of an inexact science, but the cooking of a paella is best when it's shared. So when our friends Michael and Kelly came over one year for lunch on the 4th of July, we decided that we would all bring something to throw into the pan. We called it paella by committee. The truth is that there's no really wrong way to make paella. It's the kind of thing that should be made out of what is on hand and shared with those you love.

Serves 4.

- 1 1/2 CUPS SOFRITO (RECIPE ON PREVIOUS PAGE)
- 8 STRANDS SAFFRON
- 1 QUART VEGETABLE STOCK
- 1/2 CUP DRY WHITE WINE FROM SPAIN
- 1/4 CUP OLIVE OIL
- 1 1/2 CUPS ARBORIO RICE
- 2 CUPS FINELY CHOPPED KALE
- 4 EGGS (OPTIONAL)
- 1 BUNCH GREEN ONIONS (GRILLED UNTIL WELL-MARKED BY THE GRILL GRATES)
- 1 CUP PITTED GREEN OLIVES
- 1 12-OUNCE BAG FROZEN ARTICHOKE HEARTS (DEFROSTED)
- 1 14-OUNCE CAN HEARTS OF PALM (DRAINED, SLICED)
- 1 7-OUNCE JAR ROASTED RED PEPPERS (DRAINED)
- 1 CUP CHOPPED TOMATO
- 1/4 CUP CHOPPED FLAT-LEAF PARSLEY
- 1 TABLESPOON SHERRY VINEGAR
- KOSHER SALT AND CRACKED BLACK PEPPER (TO TASTE)

First, make a sofrito according to our recipe and set it aside. Next, light your outdoor grill and preheat it to medium-high. In a medium saucepan on the grill top or side burner, warm the saffron, stock, and wine. Place the paella pan over medium-high heat on your outdoor grill and add the olive oil and rice. Toast the rice in the pan, stirring occasionally to prevent burning. Cook the rice until it's golden brown. Add the chopped kale and the sofrito. Cook over medium-high heat until the kale has wilted and most of the liquid has evaporated or been absorbed. Using a wooden spoon, push the rice mixture into an even layer. Add 1 1/2 cups of stock while being careful not to stir the rice; continue to cook until stock has been absorbed. Add more stock and continue to cook until that has been absorbed as well. The rice will need 4 to 5 additions of stock in order to use all of the liquid. You'll know the paella is ready when the rice softens and a crust begins to form on the bottom of the paella pan. This crust is called the socarrat. The entire cooking process takes about 45 minutes to an hour.

Once the rice is ready, make indentions in the rice, crack the raw eggs into the indentions, and cook until the eggs have set. Top with grilled green onions, green olives, artichoke hearts, hearts of palm, and roasted red peppers. Finish with chopped tomato, fresh herbs, and a few dashes of sherry vinegar. Add salt and pepper to taste.

NOTE: Special equipment: paella pan

ETHIOPIAN VEGETABLE PLATE

We love Ethiopian food! Besides being super-delish, it's very vegetarian-and-vegan-friendly. Most of the dishes highlight a single ingredient that's been perfectly cooked and spiced to bring out the best of what it has to offer. Our buddy Ermyias Shiberou was kind enough to run it all down for us when we asked how he makes a few of the delicious dishes he serves on the vegetable plate at Blue Nile Ethiopian Kitchen in Memphis. "It's easy," he told us with a grin. It's easy for him because he and his mother Yemiserach Sahela make these dishes day in and day out and have done so for years! We were honored to hear more about their usual process.

With his instruction, we made our own Ethiopian vegetable plate at home. The secret ingredient, as it turns out, is the raw Garlic and Ginger Paste that's added to most dishes at the end of the cook time; it gives everything such a bright, deep flavor. (Oh, please note that we aren't giving you the recipe for injera, the traditional fermented bread made from teff four. It's so good but also so difficult to make, even for the pros, and it requires a naturally fermented starter. We found that using thin slices of a whole-wheat sourdough loaf is a good stand-in for injera.)

Why not make these dishes and serve them to your friends at your next dinner party? They're filling, fast, and delicious. You'll may even get a few bonus points for creativity.

Serves 6.

- ETHIOPIAN ROASTED BEETS (RECIPE FOLLOWS)
- BERBERE-SPICED SPLIT PEAS (RECIPE FOLLOWS)
- SAUTÉED CABBAGE WITH TURMERIC (RECIPE FOLLOWS)
- 8 VERY THIN SLICES OF WHOLE WHEAT SOURDOUGH BREAD OR INJERA
- JALAPEÑO AND ROSEMARY DRESSING (RECIPE FOLLOWS)

Make beets, peas, and cabbage according to the directions. Layer slices of whole wheat sourdough bread on a large platter and add the beets, peas, and cabbage on top.

ETHIOPIAN ROASTED BEETS

- 4 MEDIUM RED BEETS
- 1 MEDIUM JALAPEÑO PEPPER (THINLY SLICED)
- 1 TABLESPOON JALAPEÑO AND ROSEMARY DRESSING (RECIPE FOLLOWS)
- 1/2 TEASPOON KOSHER SALT

Preheat your oven to 350 degrees. Place the beets in a small casserole dish, cover tightly with aluminum foil, and bake for 1 1/2 hours. Allow the beets to cool completely. Peel the skin from the beets by rubbing each with a damp paper towel just as though you're polishing it; the outer skin will rub right off.

Slice beets into 1/4-inch cubes. You should have about 2 cups of cubed beets. Toss with sliced jalapeño, Jalapeño and Rosemary Dressing, and salt. Set aside in the fridge until ready to serve. (Makes 2 cups.)

continued on next page →

BERBERE-SPICED SPLIT PEAS

- 1 TABLESPOON OLIVE OIL
- 1 CUP DICED WHITE ONION
- 1 TABLESPOON BERBERE SPICE
- 1/4 CUP TOMATO PASTE
- 1 CUP YELLOW SPLIT PEAS
- 3 1/2 CUPS WARM WATER
- KOSHER SALT (TO TASTE)
- 1 TEASPOON GARLIC AND GINGER PASTE
  (RECIPE FOLLOWS)

In a medium saucepan over medium heat, add the olive oil and onion. Cook until the edges of the onion start to brown. Add the Berbere spice and tomato paste. Continue to cook, stirring frequently, until the tomato paste turns a darker shade of red. This caramelizes the sugar in the tomato paste and imparts a deep flavor. This process should take about 10 minutes.

Add the yellow split peas and 1/3 of the water. Stir, raise the temperature to high, and bring to a boil. Once the pot is boiling, lower the heat to a simmer and cook for ten minutes. Once all the water has been absorbed, add another 1/3 of the water, stir, and cook for ten minutes. Add the last of the water and stir. Cook split peas until tender, which will be approximately 10 more minutes. Stir in the garlic and ginger paste. (Makes 3 cups.)

SAUTÉED CABBAGE WITH TURMERIC

- 1 TABLESPOON OLIVE OIL
- 1 SMALL HEAD CABBAGE
  (CORED, SLICED, ABOUT 5 CUPS)
- 1 CUP ONION (SLICED)
- 1/8 TEASPOON TURMERIC
- 1/4 TEASPOON KOSHER SALT
- 1 TEASPOON GARLIC AND GINGER
  PASTE (RECIPE FOLLOWS)

Into a large sauté pan over medium-high heat, add the oil. Once it starts to shimmer, add the cabbage and onion. Cook, stirring occasionally, until soft. This process will take about 10 minutes. Add the turmeric, salt, and Garlic and Ginger Paste. Toss to incorporate. Set aside until ready to serve. (Makes 3 cups.)

JALAPEÑO AND ROSEMARY DRESSING

- JUICE OF 1 LEMON
- 1/4 TEASPOON MINCED FRESH ROSEMARY LEAVES
- 1/4 TEASPOON MINCED JALAPEÑO PEPPER
- 1/4 TEASPOON GARLIC AND GINGER PASTE (RECIPE FOLLOWS)
- 1 TABLESPOON OLIVE OIL
- KOSHER SALT AND CRACKED BLACK PEPPER (TO TASTE)

In a small bowl, combine the lemon juice, rosemary, jalapeño, Garlic and Ginger Paste, and olive oil. Whisk together and add salt and pepper to taste. (Makes about 2 tablespoons.)

GARLIC AND GINGER PASTE

- 6 MEDIUM CLOVES GARLIC
- 1-INCH PIECE FRESH GINGER
- 1/4 TEASPOON KOSHER SALT

Using a fine microplane, grate the garlic and ginger. Mix paste together in a small bowl along with the salt. (Makes 2 tablespoons.)

STUFFED SPAGHETTI SQUASH

We use spaghetti squash as a stand-in for pasta in this dish. We figured out that it helps to have a chunky sauce since the 'noodles' are thin. Cannellini beans are a really good, nutritious addition, and whole heads of roasted garlic make for an excellent pseudo-side dish. The method we've figured out in the recipe below ensures that you're not going to end up with watery squash.

Serves 2.

- 1 LARGE SPAGHETTI SQUASH
- 2 LARGE HEADS GARLIC
- 2 TABLESPOONS OLIVE OIL (DIVIDED)
- KOSHER SALT AND CRACKED BLACK PEPPER (TO TASTE)
- 1 LARGE SHALLOT (DICED)
- 1 MEDIUM RED PEPPER (DICED)

- 2 MEDIUM CARROTS (SLICED)
- 2 MEDIUM RIBS CELERY (SLICED)
- 1 TABLESPOON ITALIAN SEASONING
- 1/2 TEASPOON CRUSHED RED PEPPER FLAKES
- 1/2 CUP WHITE WINE (LIKE PINOT GRIGIO)

- 1 15-OUNCE CAN CANNELLINI BEANS (DRAINED)
- 1 28-OUNCE CAN DICED FIRE-ROASTED TOMATOES
- 2 1-OUNCE SLICES PROVOLONE CHEESE
- 1/4 CUP CHOPPED FLAT-LEAF PARSLEY

Preheat your oven to 400 degrees. Using a large knife and an abundance of caution, slice the spaghetti squash in half lengthwise and remove the seeds by scraping them out with a spoon. Discard the seeds.

Cut the top 1/3 off of each head of garlic. Drizzle the inside of the two halves of the squash and the cut side of the heads of garlic with 1 tablespoon of the olive oil. Season the squash with salt and pepper to taste. Wrap the heads of garlic in aluminum foil and place them on a baking sheet. Place the spaghetti squash cut-side-up next to the foil-wrapped garlic and place it all into the oven. Bake for 30 minutes or until the squash begins to turn golden brown at the edges. While the squash cooks, assemble and cook the sauce.

To make the sauce, start with a large frying pan over hight heat and add the remaining tablespoon of olive oil. Once the oil shimmers, add the shallot, red pepper, carrots, and celery. Cook for 3 to 5 minutes or until the vegetables begin to brown. Add the Italian seasoning, crushed red pepper flakes, and white wine. Cook until vegetables have softened and wine has reduced, about 5 minutes. Add the beans and tomatoes. Stir to incorporate and reduce heat to a simmer. The sauce should be chunky, which will give the dish a great texture.

Remove the squash from the oven and scrape the spaghetti squash up with a fork. This is easily done with a cooked squash. You'll notice that as you scrape, the squash comes up in tiny ribbons like pasta, hence the name! Season the squash with salt and pepper. Divide the sauce between the two halves and cover each with a slice of provolone. The heat from the sauce will melt the cheese, but feel free to place it under a broiler for a minute or two on high to get it melty and bubbly. Garnish the squash with chopped parsley. Add salt and pepper to taste and serve alongside the roasted garlic.

SPICY AVOCADO SUSHI ROLLS

Making a beautiful platter of sushi at home has been a Valentine's Day tradition for us ever since we first started dating. On the side, we'll include a salad with ginger dressing (see page 204 for a grilled version) and tofu spring rolls with spicy peanut sauce.

Honestly, if we can make sushi, anyone can do it! There's no need to feel intimidated. We called in an expert to give us some help with this one: Marisa Baggett, author of *Vegetarian Sushi Secrets: 101 Healthy and Delicious Recipes* (Tuttle, 2016). She also let us in on her secret to perfect sushi rice.

Makes 4 rolls, 20 pieces.

- 4 4 X 7-INCH SHEETS NORI
- 3 CUPS PREPARED BASIC SUSHI RICE (RECIPE FOLLOWS)
- 4 TEASPOONS RED PEPPER JELLY
- 2 TEASPOONS WHITE SESAME SEEDS (TOASTED)
- 2 GREEN ONIONS (THINLY SLICED)
- 1 MEDIUM AVOCADO (PEELED, CUT INTO 8 WEDGES)
- 1 MEDIUM CARROT (PEELED, CUT INTO MATCHSTICKS)
- 8 LARGE SHISO OR BASIL LEAVES

Prepare the Basic Sushi Rice according the the recipe. Place a 4 x 7-inch sheet of nori vertically on a bamboo rolling mat. Make sure that the short end is parallel to the bottom of the mat and that the rough side is facing upwards. Dip your fingertips lightly in cool water and spread about 3/4 cup of prepared sushi rice evenly over the bottom 3/4 of the nori.

Spread 1 teaspoon of red pepper jelly across the center of the rice. Sprinkle 1/2 teaspoon of white sesame seeds over the rice followed by 1/4 of the green onions. Arrange 2 wedges of avocado across the center of the sushi rice; make sure they extend to both edges of the nori. Lay 1/4 of the carrots in a neat line above the avocado. Top with 2 shiso leaves.

Wet your fingertips again and slide your thumbs underneath the mat while grasping the fillings with all other fingertips. Roll the bottom of the mat just over the fillings, tucking the fillings tightly under the fold. (Don't allow the mat to get stuck inside the roll!) Lift the edge of the mat. Continue rolling until the roll is completely sealed and the seam is facing down. Gently shape the roll by pressing your forefingers on top of the mat while simultaneously pressing your thumbs and middle fingers on the sides. Allow the roll to rest seam-side-down on a cutting board for at least 2 minutes. Repeat with remaining nori, sushi rice, and fillings.

To cut the roll, dip the blade of a very sharp knife in water. Use a swift sawing motion to cut the roll into 5 pieces. Serve with soy sauce for dipping.

continued on next page →

BASIC SUSHI RICE

- 1 1/4 CUPS SHORT-GRAIN WHITE RICE
- 1 1/4 CUPS WATER
- 1/4 CUP SUSHI RICE DRESSING
  (RECIPE FOLLOWS)

Cover the rice with cool water in a medium bowl. Gently swish the rice in a circular motion with your hands while taking care not to break the grains apart. Pour the water off and repeat three times. Place the rice in a fine mesh strainer and rinse it with cool water. The run-off water should begin to look clear. Allow the rice to drain in the strainer for 10 minutes.

Place the rice and measured water in a rice cooker. Once you've started the rice cooker, cook the rice for exactly 40 minutes. Most likely, the cooker will indicate that the rice is done before 40 minutes have elapsed, but be patient. Do not lift the lid or stop the process before the time is up.

(Alternately, if you don't have a rice cooker, you may bring the water to a boil in a large soup pot. Once the water is boiling, add the rice, place a lid on the pot, and reduce heat to medium-low. Allow rice to cook for 40 minutes.)

While the rice cooks, place a wooden spoon or rice paddle in a shallow bowl of water to soak. This will prevent the cooked rice from sticking to the paddle while you toss it with the Sushi Rice Dressing. Place the steamed rice onto a large, flat cutting board. With the soaked wooden spoon or paddle, gently 'cut' the rice into pieces like you would cut a pie. Pour 1/4 cup of the Sushi Rice Dressing over the rice and toss well. Continue adding the Sushi Rice Dressing in 1/4 cup intervals to the rice, tossing well after each addition. Spread the rice into a thin layer and let it cool for 10 minutes. Gently flip the rice over with the soaked wooden spoon or paddle and let it cool for 5 minutes. Place the rice in a large non-metal bowl or container and cover with a damp, lint-free dishcloth until ready for use. (Makes about 3 cups.)

SUSHI RICE DRESSING

- 1/4 CUP RICE VINEGAR
- 1 TABLESPOON AND
  1 HEAPING TEASPOON SUGAR
- 1 TEASPOON SEA SALT

In a small non-metal bowl, mix together the rice vinegar, sugar, and salt. Whisk it vigorously for about 2 minutes or until most of the unrefined sugar and salt dissolve. Set it aside until ready for use. Allow mixture to reach room temperature before use. (Makes about 1/4 cup.)

CAPRESE PIE

We love making tomato pie in the summer, and this version is a mash-up between Southern tomato pie and Italian caprese salad with a nod to Margherita pizza. If you want to leave out the dairy to make it vegan, you may substitute a drained and sliced block of extra-firm tofu. Believe it or don't, the flavor of fresh Buffalo mozzarella and tofu are actually very similar. Tofu is made using the same process as cheesemaking. so it makes sense that they share many of the same textures and flavors.

Whichever way you choose to make it, it'll be wonderful! Serve this to dinner guests for an easy make-ahead meal or keep it all to yourself and relish the leftovers.

Serves 4-6.

- 1 STORE-BOUGHT FROZEN PIE CRUST
- 3 LARGE TOMATOES (BEEFSTEAK, JET STAR, OR BETTER BOY)
- 1/2 TEASPOON KOSHER SALT
- 1/4 CUP BALSAMIC VINEGAR
- 1 1/2 TEASPOONS OLIVE OIL
- 2 CUPS BASIL LEAVES
- 12 OUNCES FRESH BUFFALO MOZZARELLA CHEESE (SLICED INTO 1/4-INCH ROUNDS)
- KOSHER SALT AND CRACKED BLACK PEPPER (TO TASTE)

Preheat your oven to 350 degrees and bake the pie crust until golden brown. This should take about 12 to 15 minutes, but please refer to the package instructions for guidance. While the crust is baking, prepare the tomatoes and the dressing.

Core the tomatoes and slice them into generous 1/4-inch slices. (You should get 4 to 6 slices per tomato.) Layer tomato slices and salt into a large bowl, and make sure to get a little salt on each slice. Allow salted tomatoes to rest for 20 minutes. You'll notice quite a bit of liquid collected at the bottom of the bowl. Remove tomato slices and place them between two clean kitchen towels until you're ready to assemble the dish. This process ensures that the pie won't be watery. Discard the tomato water in the bowl.

In a small saucepan over medium heat, add the balsamic vinegar and cook until reduced by half. It will become thick and syrupy when it's ready. Remove from heat and add the olive oil.

Assemble the pie in the shell by shingling in a tomato slice, basil leaf, and then a piece of mozzarella in a circular pattern following the shape of the crust. Once you get all the way around the pie, start another layer on top of that. Using your hands, lightly press the tomatoes, basil, and cheese down into the crust. This will make the finished pie more compact and easier to cut. Drizzle the top of the pie with the reduced balsamic and olive oil dressing. Refrigerate for 30 minutes before serving. Season with salt and pepper to taste.

SOUPS, SALADS & SIDES

. . . .

MULLIGATAWNY: AN INDIAN-INSPIRED VEGETABLE STEW

Here we've included a simple-but-hugely-flavorful homemade curry paste that easily comes together in the work bowl of your food processor. We stumbled upon this method while developing a vegetarian gumbo recipe and thought it would work well for mulligatawny—and it does! We ate this stew for dinner one night, lunch the next day, and then had it with a poached egg on top for breakfast the following morning. That's how good it is.

Serves 6.

- 1 MEDIUM ONION (ROUGHLY CHOPPED)
- 2-INCH PIECE FRESH GINGER
- 8 CLOVES GARLIC (PEELED)
- 1 MEDIUM TOMATO (CORED)
- 2 TABLESPOONS CURRY POWDER
- 1 TEASPOON CORIANDER
- 1 TEASPOON CUMIN
- 1/2 TEASPOON CINNAMON
- 1 TABLESPOON SAMBAL
- 1 TABLESPOON SUGAR
- 1 TABLESPOON WHITE VINEGAR

- 1 1/2 TABLESPOONS UNSALTED BUTTER
- 1/2 CUP LENTILS
- 3 CUPS VEGETABLE BROTH (MORE IF NEEDED)
- 1 TABLESPOON SOY SAUCE (LIKE BRAGG® LIQUID AMINOS)
- 1/2 CUP CHOPPED DRIED CHERRIES
- 1 MEDIUM RUSSET POTATO (PEELED AND DICED)
- 1 MEDIUM GREEN BELL PEPPER (DICED)

- 1 MEDIUM HEAD OF CAULIFLOWER (BROKEN INTO FLORETS)
- 4-5 MEDIUM CARROTS (DICED)
- 1 13.5-OUNCE CAN COCONUT MILK
- KOSHER SALT AND CRACKED BLACK PEPPER (TO TASTE)
- 1 CUP SALTED WHOLE CASHEWS (TO GARNISH)
- 1/2 CUP CILANTRO LEAVES (TO GARNISH)
- RICE (OPTIONAL)
- WHOLE WHEAT NAAN (OPTIONAL; PAGE 258)

Into a food processor, place the onion, ginger, garlic, tomato, curry powder, coriander, cumin, cinnamon, sambal, sugar, and vinegar. Blend until a loose paste forms and all ingredients are throughly combined.

In a large soup pot or Dutch oven over medium-high heat, melt the butter and add the curry paste. Cook, stirring frequently, until most of the moisture has evaporated and the paste becomes very thick. Add

the lentils, broth, and soy sauce. Stir, cover, and allow the mixture to cook for 10 minutes to soften the lentils. Add the cherries, potato, bell pepper, cauliflower, carrots, and coconut milk. Add salt and pepper to taste.

Cover and reduce heat to a simmer. Cook until the vegetables are tender. Serve garnished with cashews and cilantro leaves and, if you like, add rice and a side of naan.

APPLE-PARSNIP SOUP

Parsnips look like pale carrots, something Bunnicula might've gotten ahold of and completely drained of color. They have a spicy bite of flavor and taste earthy and bright, a little bit like mild horseradish. They've started showing up more and more starting in the fall, and we think they're great when paired with apples.

Serves 2.

- 1 WHITE ONION (DICED)
- 1 TEASPOON UNSALTED BUTTER
- 1 CUP SPARKLING WHITE WINE
- 2 LARGE PARSNIPS (PEELED, ROUGHLY CHOPPED)
- 2 LARGE HONEYCRISP APPLES (PEELED, ROUGHLY CHOPPED)
- 1 WHITE SWEET POTATO (PEELED, ROUGHLY CHOPPED)
- 1 TEASPOON RUBBED SAGE
- PINCH OF KOSHER SALT
- 1 CUP HALF AND HALF
- WATER
- GREEN ONIONS AND SHREDDED WHITE CHEDDAR (TO GARNISH)

Sauté the onions in the butter until translucent and then add the wine. Allow the mixture to reduce. Add the parsnips, apple, potato, and sage to the mixture. Add a pinch of salt. Cover and cook for about 10 minutes or until vegetables have softened and have taken on a slight color. Reduce the heat and add the half-and-half. Do not allow soup to boil after adding the cream as it could curdle. Using an immersion blender, blend the mixture until smooth. Add enough water to achieve the consistency you desire. Garnish with sliced green onion and shredded white cheddar.

SPICY TOMATO AND CASHEW BISQUE

This soup is one of those things that we'd usually just whip up on a whim at home and not immediately think about putting out there as a recipe. It almost seems too easy, but there are some solid ideas here that are worth a mention.

This is a simple tomato soup recipe made with fresh carrots, onions, and celery. The creaminess of the soup comes from cashews, not dairy. It's delicious and wholesome, and it packs a good bit of protein due to the cashews.

Serves 4.

- 1 TABLESPOON OLIVE OIL
- 1 ONION (DICED)
- 2 CARROTS (DICED)
- 2 RIBS CELERY (DICED)
- 3 CLOVES GARLIC (CRUSHED)
- 1 TEASPOON CORIANDER
- 1/2 TEASPOON CRUSHED RED PEPPER
- 1 28-OUNCE CAN FIRE-ROASTED TOMATOES
- 3 1/2 CUPS VEGETABLE BROTH
- 1 HEAPING CUP ROASTED CASHEWS
- KOSHER SALT AND CRACKED BLACK PEPPER (TO TASTE)
- SRIRACHA HOT SAUCE AND CHOPPED CHIVES (TO GARNISH)

In a large soup pot or Dutch oven over medium-high heat, add the olive oil and the onion, carrots, celery, and garlic. Cook, stirring often until vegetables have softened and are staring to brown, about 8 minutes. Add the coriander and crushed red pepper and cook for another minute. Add the tomatoes, broth, and cashews. Reduce to a simmer, cover and cook for 10 to 15 minutes or until the vegetables are soft. Using an immersion blender, blend soup until smooth; this may take a few minutes. Alternately, use a food processor, but be careful and allow for airflow with a towel on top of the lid that has the middle cap removed.

Taste and add salt and pepper to your liking. Serve the soup garnished with Sriracha (if you want a little more heat) and chives.

VEGETARIAN MATZO BALL SOUP

This soup has been in rotation at our house for 15 years or so. It has survived every culinary trend and our always-changing ideas about what we should or shouldn't be eating. We can even remember making this soup almost twenty years ago in our first Midtown Memphis apartment in a ridiculously minuscule kitchen.

So why does this dish have such staying power? It's hearty, delicious, and so simple to make. We utilize a box mix and use extra virgin olive oil in place of the vegetable oil that's recommended in the instructions. We also cook the vegetable components separate from the matzo balls, so they retain some of their sturdiness and don't turn to mush as they cook.

Serves 2.

- 1 4.5-OUNCE BOX MATZO BALL MIX
- 1/4 CUP OLIVE OIL
- 2 LARGE EGGS (BEATEN)
- 1 QUART VEGETABLE BROTH
- 2 BAY LEAVES
- 4 SPRIGS THYME

- 1 TABLESPOON UNSALTED BUTTER
- 2 RIBS CELERY (DICED)
- 1 LARGE CARROT (DICED)
- 1 LARGE SHALLOT (FINELY DICED)

- 1/2 CUP WHITE WINE (LIKE PINOT GRIGIO)
- 2 TABLESPOONS CHOPPED FRESH PARSLEY
- KOSHER SALT AND CRACKED BLACK PEPPER (TO TASTE)

Make the matzo ball mix according to the package instructions, which call for vegetable oil (use olive oil instead) and 2 large eggs. Set the mixture aside in the fridge for 15 to 20 minutes.

In a medium saucepan over medium-high heat, bring the broth, bay leaves, and thyme to a boil. Remove the chilled matzo ball mix from the fridge. Using a 1-tablespoon-size ice cream scoop, drop the mix into the boiling broth one at a time. Lower the heat to a simmer. Secure the lid and simmer for 30 minutes. Do not lift the lid during the cooking time; this is one of the secrets to ending up with fluffy matzo balls.

In a large frying pan over medium-high heat, melt the butter and add the diced celery, carrots, and shallots. Once they start to caramelize, deglaze the pan with the white wine and cook until most of the liquid has evaporated. Set aside until ready to serve.

To serve, place 3 to 4 matzo balls into a bowl, ladle on enough broth to almost cover the matzo balls about halfway, add 1/4 of the vegetable mixture into the bowl, and garnish with chopped parsley, salt, and pepper.

VEGETARIAN SHIITAKE RAMEN

Ramen is one of those easy-to-make vegetarian meals that you can fix in minutes. The key here is the vegetarian broth, which employs kombu and dried shiitake to give it body and flavor. Due mostly to the hearty broth, this version doesn't actually taste vegetarian....hey, mission accomplished!

Serves 2.

- 1 TABLESPOON TOASTED SESAME OIL
- 4 OUNCES FRESH BABY SHIITAKE MUSHROOMS
- CRACKED BLACK PEPPER (TO TASTE)
- 1 TABLESPOON PONZU
- 2 2.8-OUNCE PACKAGES INSTANT RAMEN NOODLES (COOKED ACCORDING TO PACKAGE INSTRUCTIONS; DISCARD THE FLAVOR PACKETS)
- 1 MEDIUM CARROT (SHRED USING A SERRATED PEELER)
- 2 SOFT-BOILED EGGS (SEE NOTE BELOW)
- 1 GREEN ONION (THINLY SLICED)
- SHIITAKE RAMEN BROTH (RECIPE FOLLOWS)

In a medium pan over high heat, add the sesame oil and the shiitake mushrooms stem-side-up. Season with plenty of pepper. Sear the mushrooms for 2 to 3 minutes or until nicely browned. Add the ponzu and toss until the liquid has evaporated; this happens quickly. Remove the mushrooms from the pan and set aside until ready to assemble the dish.

To assemble the soup, divide the noodles between two bowls. Into each bowl, place half of the mushrooms off to the side of the pile of noodles and half the carrots off to the other side. Top the mound of noodles with the soft-boiled egg and garnish with the onion. Pour in enough hot broth to cover the noodles about halfway.

NOTE: Bring salted water to a full boil, lower the eggs into the water, pull them out 6 minutes later, and place them into an ice bath. Wait until eggs are cool to the touch and then peel and serve.

SHIITAKE RAMEN BROTH

- 1 QUART LOW-SODIUM VEGETABLE BROTH
- 3 GREEN ONIONS (WHITE AND GREEN PARTS, ROUGHLY CHOPPED)
- 1 CUP DRIED SHIITAKE MUSHROOMS
- 12 X 3-INCH PIECE KOMBU (RINSED BRIEFLY UNDER COLD WATER)
- 4 CLOVES GARLIC (CRUSHED)
- 2 TEASPOONS SOY SAUCE (LIKE BRAGG® LIQUID AMINOS)
- 2 TEASPOONS MIRIN

Place the broth, onions, mushrooms, kombu, garlic, soy sauce, and mirin in a medium saucepan and turn the heat on high. Once the mixture begins to boil, reduce the heat and continue to cook until the mixture has reduced by more than half; this should take 20 to 30 minutes. Strain the broth using a mesh strainer, and make sure to press all of the liquid out from the mushrooms and kombu. Keep warm until ready to use. (Makes 1 1/2 cups.)

VEGETARIAN TOM YUM SOUP

Anytime we eat Thai food, we longingly stare at the Tom Yum Soup on the menu. It contains shrimp stock and chicken stock—it's just how that soup is made. So, we decided to take matters into our own hands and come up with a great vegetarian version of this classic.

Kombu is the key here. It's a sea vegetable, and it has the most umami of any vegetable. The role of the shrimp, a classic component of this soup, is being played by king oyster mushrooms, which have a very seafood-like texture and flavor. These elements paired with the fragrant punch of the broth, the spiciness of the sambal, and the acidity of the lime make for one beautiful bowl of soup.

Serves 2.

- 2 STALKS LEMONGRASS
- 1 QUART LOW-SODIUM VEGETABLE BROTH
- 3 LIME LEAVES
- 1/2-INCH PIECE FRESH GINGER (SLICED)
- 1/2 OUNCE KOMBU (ABOUT 3 SMALL SHEETS, RINSED)

- 1 TABLESPOON LIGHT BROWN SUGAR
- 1 TABLESPOON SAMBAL
- 2 TABLESPOONS VEGETARIAN FISH SAUCE (PAGE 254) OR SOY SAUCE (LIKE BRAGG® LIQUID AMINOS)
- 4 CLOVES GARLIC (CRUSHED)

- 1 CUP TOMATO WEDGES
- 1 RED PEPPER (SLICED)
- 1 CUP COCONUT MILK
- 1 1/2 CUPS SLICED AND QUARTERED KING OYSTER MUSHROOMS
- 1/2 CUP FRESH CILANTRO
- 1 LIME (QUARTERED)

Trim the ends off of the lemongrass and peel away the first two layers. With the back of your knife or a frying pan, beat the lemongrass until it splinters. Cut into 4 pieces and set aside. In a large saucepan, bring the broth to a boil with the lemongrass, lime leaves, ginger, kombu, brown sugar, fish sauce (or soy sauce), and garlic. Cover and reduce the heat to a simmer; allow this mixture to cook for 20 to 25 minutes. Strain out the solids, leaving only a fragrant broth. Return the broth to the saucepan over medium heat. Add the tomato, red pepper, and coconut milk. Allow the tomato and pepper to warm through. Just before serving, stir in the king oyster mushrooms; know that they're easy to overcook and become rubbery if they sit in the hot broth for too long. Ladle the soup into bowls and garnish with cilantro and a squeeze of lime.

CASHEW NOODLE SALAD

If you are what you eat, then it's likely that we're about 15% cashew noodle salad. We've been having it for lunch at least once a week since we were kids. The version we love so much is an old Squash Blossom grocery recipe that's still served at our Memphis Whole Foods today. Legend has it that it was taken off the menu once, and customers protested so much that it was returned to the deli case, where it rightfully belongs.

Our version of it is a bit spicier than the original. We sometimes dress it up for dinner with a few simple tofu and mushroom skewers.

Serves 2.

- 1 CUP CASHEWS
- 1/4 CUP SOY SAUCE (LIKE BRAGG® LIQUID AMINOS)
- 2 TABLESPOONS SAMBAL
- 1/4 CUP SESAME OIL
- 1/4 CUP MIRIN

- 1/4 CUP RICE VINEGAR
- 1 CLOVE GARLIC
- 2 GREEN ONIONS (CHOPPED)
- 1 8-OUNCE BOX DRY SPAGHETTI OR SOBA NOODLES (COOKED, RINSED, AND COOLED)

- CASHEWS, CILANTRO, GREEN ONION (CHOPPED) (TO GARNISH)

Place the cashews, soy sauce, sambal, sesame oil, mirin, rice vinegar, and garlic into the food processor and blend until smooth. Toss the cashew dressing and green onions with the cooked and cooled noodles. Garnish each serving with cashews, cilantro, and more green onion.

VEGAN AVOCADO AND HEIRLOOM TOMATO CAPRESE

Here's a simple side dish to add to your outdoor summer party rotation. If you're like us, you might've already figured out your main dish ahead of time, but then you get that nagging feeling that you need something else, something special that everyone will really like. We've got you covered with this Caprese salad with a Mexican twist. The avocados stand in for the typical buffalo mozzarella, and cilantro takes the place of fresh basil.

Serves 4.

- 2 MEDIUM HEIRLOOM TOMATOES (CUT INTO 1/4-INCH SLICES)
- 2 MEDIUM AVOCADOS (PITTED, PEELED, AND CUT INTO 1/4-INCH SLICES)
- 1 TABLESPOON OLIVE OIL
- 1 TEASPOON CHAMPAGNE VINEGAR
- 1 SERRANO PEPPER (THINLY SLICED)
- 1/4 CUP FRESH CILANTRO LEAVES
- KOSHER SALT AND CRACKED BLACK PEPPER (TO TASTE)
- 1 LIME (QUARTERED)

On a serving platter, arrange the salad by alternating the slices of tomato and avocado. Drizzle with the olive oil and then the vinegar. Add sliced Serrano pepper, cilantro leaves, and salt and pepper to taste. Serve lime wedges on the side to be squeezed over the dish.

FRESH CUCUMBER NOODLES WITH CASHEWS AND MINT

Here in the South, we are completely overrun with cucumbers in the summertime. So this is a new idea that'll have you scooping up all the cucumbers you can get your hands on this year. Spiralize them and turn them into spaghetti-like noodles! This cold, spicy dish goes great alongside sushi or curry. Best of all, it comes together with no cooking at all and only takes a few minutes to make.

Serves 2.

- 1 LARGE ENGLISH CUCUMBER (ABOUT 14 INCHES)
- 1 SMALL SERRANO PEPPER (VERY THINLY SLICED)
- 1 TEASPOON GRATED FRESH GINGER
- 1 TEASPOON SOY SAUCE (LIKE BRAGG® LIQUID AMINOS)
- 1/2 TEASPOON PLUM VINEGAR
- 1 TEASPOON MIRIN
- 1/2 TEASPOON SESAME OIL
- 1/2 CUP MINT LEAVES
- 1/2 CUP CRUSHED CASHEWS
- 1 TABLESPOON SLICED CHIVES

Run the cucumber through a spiralizer or break it down using a serrated peeler. (Alternately, it would be just fine to thinly slice the cucumber or to cut it into matchsticks.)

In a large bowl, toss the cucumber, Serrano pepper, ginger, soy, vinegar, mirin, and sesame oil together until everything is well-coated. Place onto a plate to serve family-style or divide between two bowls for individual servings. Garnish with mint, cashews, and chives.

NOTE: Special equipment: a spiralizer

SIMPLE RAITA

- 1/2 CUP FINELY DICED ENGLISH CUCUMBER
- KOSHER SALT (TO TASTE)
- JUICE OF 1/2 LIME
- 3/4 CUP GREEK YOGURT

In a medium bowl, mix the cucumber, salt, lime, and yogurt. Set aside in the fridge until ready to use. (Makes about 1 1/4 cups.)

HERBED DRESSING

- 1 CUP MIXED FRESH HERBS
  (LIKE BASIL, MINT, PARSLEY, CILANTRO)
- 1/4 CUP OLIVE OIL
- JUICE FROM 1 LIME

Using an immersion blender or your food processor, blend the herbs, oil, lime juice, and garlic until smooth. Season with salt and pepper. Set aside until you're ready to dress the salad. (Makes about 3/4 cup.)

CURRIED ACORN SQUASH SALAD WITH APPLES

We created this dish for a first course at the Garden Harvest benefit dinner at St. Jude Children's Research Hospital in our hometown of Memphis. It's always so meaningful to be working with and learning from talented chefs for a cause that's close to our hearts, getting to be creative, and sharing our take on vegetarian food. Think of this memorable salad as a deconstructed curry dish that's just right for the fall season.

Serves 6.

- 2 MEDIUM ACORN SQUASHES
- 1 TABLESPOON OLIVE OIL
- 1 TABLESPOON CURRY POWDER (RECIPE FOLLOWS)
- KOSHER SALT AND CRACKED BLACK PEPPER (TO TASTE)

- SIMPLE RAITA (RECIPE ON PREVIOUS PAGE)
- HERBED DRESSING (RECIPE ON PREVIOUS PAGE)
- 1 APPLE (LIKE A PINK LADY OR A HONEYCRISP)

- 2 CUPS ARUGULA
- 1 SHALLOT (THINLY SLICED)

Preheat your oven to 400 degrees. Cut the stem end off of each acorn squash and scoop out the seeds; discard them. Slice both acorn squashes in half and then cut the halves into 1/2-inch to 3/4-inch slices. In a large bowl, toss the slices with the olive oil and then the curry powder, salt, and pepper. On a parchment-lined baking sheet, arrange the squash slices in a single layer and roast for 20 minutes or until the edges start to caramelize. Remove and allow to cool.

Make the Simple Raita and Herbed Dressing according to the recipes. Cut the apple into matchsticks and set aside. Place a layer of roasted squash on a large serving platter and top it with the Simple Raita. Add the arugula, shallots, and apples before drizzling the dish with Herbed Dressing.

CURRY POWDER

- 1 TEASPOON GROUND GINGER
- 1/2 TEASPOON GRANULATED GARLIC
- SEEDS FROM 4 CARDAMOM PODS
- 1/4 TEASPOON CLOVE
- 1 TEASPOON CINNAMON
- 1 TEASPOON GROUND TURMERIC
- 1 TEASPOON CUMIN

- 1 TEASPOON CORIANDER SEED
- 1 TEASPOON HOT CHILI POWDER (OR TO TASTE)

Mix all ingredients in a small bowl and then run them through the spice grinder for a few seconds to break down the cardamom seeds. This mix will keep for up to a year in a sealed container. (Makes about 2 1/2 tablespoons.)

THE VEGETARIAN BBQ 'BOSS MAN' SALAD WITH YOGURT RANCH DRESSING

The Germantown Commissary is a fixture in the old town square of a suburb right outside of Memphis. Amy's partial to their banana pudding, and somehow, before she could drive, she'd often find a way to go up to the Commissary by herself and order it. My standard order was a bit strange for a kid: I'd always order a salad. Granted, this was a huge salad named the 'Boss Man,' and it was covered in pulled pork and served with a thick ranch dressing. It was, to my nine-year-old self, pure heaven.

I wanted to figure out a way to celebrate that dish, but also to update it for how we like to eat now. The result, a mixture of crunchy lettuce, smoky eggplant, and rich dressing, is our take on a Memphis classic that's big enough to be the boss.

Serves 2.

- 2 MEDIUM ITALIAN EGGPLANTS
- 2 TABLESPOONS OLIVE OIL
- 1 TABLESPOON TOASTED SESAME OIL
- 1 TABLESPOON CHAMPAGNE VINEGAR

- 2 TABLESPOONS OF THE CHUBBY VEGETARIAN'S SIGNATURE MEMPHIS DRY RUB (PAGE 252)
- 1 HEAD OF ROMAINE LETTUCE (CHOPPED)
- 1 MEDIUM CARROT (SHREDDED)

- 1 CUP SHREDDED PURPLE CABBAGE
- 1 SMALL CUCUMBER (THINLY SLICED)
- 1 LARGE TOMATO (SLICED AND QUARTERED)
- YOGURT RANCH DRESSING (RECIPE FOLLOWS)
- 1 CUP OF BBQ SAUCE (WARMED)

YOGURT RANCH DRESSING

- 1/2 CUP GREEK YOGURT
- JUICE OF 1/2 LEMON
- KOSHER SALT AND CRACKED BLACK PEPPER (TO TASTE)
- 1 TABLESPOON MINCED FRESH DILL
- 1 TABLESPOON MINCED FRESH CHIVES

- 1 TABLESPOON MINCED FRESH PARSLEY
- 1 TABLESPOON OLIVE OIL

In a medium bowl, whisk together the yogurt, lemon juice, salt, pepper, dill, chives, parsley, and olive oil. Set aside in the fridge until ready to use. (Makes about 3/4 cup of dressing.)

Preheat your outdoor grill to high. Prepare the eggplants by slicing each in half longways, and then cut slits in the flesh of the eggplant every 1/4 inch; cut through most of the flesh, but not the skin.

In a medium bowl, whisk together the olive oil, sesame oil, and vinegar. Drizzle each eggplant half with the oil and vinegar mixture. Apply The Chubby Vegetarian's Signature Memphis Dry Rub liberally to each eggplant.

Place the eggplant skin-side-down on the hot grill and close the lid for 20 minutes. Remove the eggplant and tent with foil. Allow it to cool so that you're able to handle it.

While you're waiting for the eggplant to cool, prepare the salad by tossing together the romaine, shredded carrot, shredded cabbage, cucumber, and tomatoes. Prepare the Yogurt Ranch Dressing according to the recipe.

Now, using your hands, pull as much of the eggplant flesh away from the skin while keeping the large strands intact. Discard the skin. Toss the eggplant with the warm BBQ sauce. Divide the salad among two plates—it'll be a big serving—and top each salad with a heap of BBQ eggplant. Include the Yogurt Ranch Dressing on the side.

KALE CAESAR SALAD WITH SEARED ARTICHOKE HEARTS

This salad is super simple and really delicious, a combination that works well for us most days. As you've likely experienced, most salads wilt into bunch of nothing once they're dressed. This one is different: it improves over time and is even better the next day because kale is just that hearty.

Serves 4.

- 1 LARGE HEAD CURLY KALE (STEMS REMOVED, ABOUT 10 CUPS)
- JUICE OF 1 LEMON
- 1 TEASPOON GRAINY MUSTARD (LIKE ZATARAIN'S®)
- 2 TABLESPOONS MAYONNAISE

- 1 CLOVE GARLIC (MINCED)
- 1 TEASPOON VEGETARIAN WORCESTERSHIRE SAUCE
- 1 TEASPOON HONEY
- 1/2 CUP GRATED PARMIGIANO-REGGIANO CHEESE

- 1 TABLESPOON OLIVE OIL
- 1 14-OUNCE CAN ARTICHOKE HEART QUARTERS (IN WATER, DRAINED)
- 3 CUPS CROUTONS (SEE NOTE BELOW)

In a large non-reactive glass bowl, massage the kale with the lemon juice; next, tear the leaves with your hands until they're in bite-sized pieces. In a small bowl, whisk together the mustard, mayonnaise, garlic, Worcestershire, and honey. Add this and half of the cheese to the kale and toss to incorporate. Allow it to sit covered in the fridge for a couple of hours; the acid in the lemon will soften the kale. Add salt and pepper to taste once you're ready to serve. Place the mixture into a large bowl or divide onto 4 plates.

In a large frying pan over high heat, add the olive oil. Once the oil starts to shimmer, toss in the drained artichoke hearts and cook until browned; turn once.

Place the warm artichoke hearts onto the kale, along with the croutons and the remaining cheese. Store any leftovers in an airtight container for up to 3 days.

NOTE: Make your own croutons by cubing the bread of your choice, drizzling it with 1 tablespoon of olive oil and placing it into a 250-degree oven until dry and crisp. A French or Italian loaf works well for this, but you can also use gluten-free bread like we often do. Add extra flavor if you like by adding in an Italian herb mix or garlic powder to the bread before toasting.

GRILLED ROMAINE SALAD WITH FRESH GINGER DRESSING

So this is our version of a salad that's available in some form or another at almost any Japanese restaurant in America. Our ginger dressing is smooth and flavorful, and it's a perfect complement to the smoky grilled romaine lettuce. While it's pretty close to perfect on this particular salad, it's also great on spring rolls or tossed in with some stir-fried vegetables or drizzled over rice noodles. Consider it an all-purpose food enhancer.

Serves 2.

- 2 HEADS ROMAINE LETTUCE (SPLIT LENGTHWISE)
- 1 1/2 CUPS GRAPE OR CHERRY TOMATOES (HALVED)
- 1/2 CUP SLICED ALMONDS (TOASTED)
- 1/4 CUP SLICED GREEN ONION
- FRESH GINGER DRESSING (RECIPE FOLLOWS)
- KOSHER SALT AND CRACKED BLACK PEPPER (TO TASTE)

Heat a cast-iron grill pan over high heat. Sear the cut side of each head of romaine until it's nicely marked; this should take about 2 minutes. Dress each salad with grape tomatoes, sliced almonds, green onions, and the Fresh Ginger Dressing. Add salt and pepper to taste.

FRESH GINGER DRESSING

- 1 1/2-INCH PIECE FRESH GINGER (PEELED)
- 1 CLOVE GARLIC
- 1 TABLESPOON SUGAR
- 2 TABLESPOONS SOY SAUCE (OR BRAGG® LIQUID AMINOS)
- 1 TABLESPOON BROWN RICE VINEGAR
- 1/4 CUP OLIVE OIL
- CRACKED BLACK PEPPER (TO TASTE)

Place the ginger, garlic, sugar, soy sauce, brown rice vinegar, and oil into the work cup of your immersion blender or food processor. Blend until it's very smooth and the oil has emulsified. Add pepper to taste. (Makes about 1/2 cup.)

CHIPOTLE ELOTE SALAD

This incredible salad gets a ton of extra flavor from a homemade chipotle aioli rather than just the usual plain old mayonnaise. Best of all, it's fast—especially if you use organic frozen corn, which is the best corn you can get if doesn't happen to be summertime.

Serves 4.

- 1 CLOVE GARLIC (PEELED)
- 1/4 CUP MAYONNAISE

- JUICE FROM 1/2 LIME
- 1 TO 2 CHIPOTLE CHILIES FROM A CAN

- 5 EARS OF CORN
- 1 CUP FINELY CRUMBLED COTIJA CHEESE (USE THE FOOD PROCESSOR)

Into the work bowl of your food processor, mini-prep, or immersion blender cup, add the garlic, mayonnaise, lime juice, and chipotle chilies. Blend until smooth. Set aside.

Turn the broiler of your oven on high. Place the corn on a baking sheet and place under the broiler for about 10 minutes. Turn the corn every 3 minutes or until the sugars begin to caramelize and the corn starts to become lightly browned on the side that's facing up. Remove from the oven and allow to cool. Cut the kernels of corn from the cob. Combine with the mayonnaise mixture and the cheese. Serve warm.

NICOISE SALAD

When we first had this type of salad, we were visiting family in Seattle on a gorgeous summer day. We walked to a patio by a bike path, a bridge, and the ocean, and we ate lunch and caught up on just about everything. That Nicoise salad was perfect: green and fresh with tons of flavor and a tart, lemony dressing. We resolved then and there to order this same salad anytime we saw it again on a menu. And then we started wondering: *How would we make a vegetarian version of it at home?*

We switched out the tuna for artichokes and added some green lentils, but we kept the balance of the salad pretty classic. Present it rustically on a big platter and let folks serve themselves, or make petite and pretty salads with a smaller chop—your choice.

Serves 4.

- FRENCH GREEN LENTILS (RECIPE FOLLOWS)
- 1 LARGE POT OF SALTED WATER (AS SALTY AS THE SEA)
- 1/4 CUP OLD BAY SEASONING
- 1/2 POUND HARICOTS VERTS (OR GREEN BEANS)
- 2 MEDIUM ARTICHOKES

- 1 LEMON (HALVED)
- 6 MEDIUM RED NEW POTATOES (QUARTERED)
- 4 LARGE EGGS
- 1 HEAD BUTTER LETTUCE (CUT AWAY FROM THE CORE)
- 2 CUPS HALVED GRAPE TOMATOES

- 1 CUP NICOISE OLIVES
- 4 TO 8 CAPER BERRIES
- THYME AND TARRAGON DRESSING (RECIPE FOLLOWS)
- KOSHER SALT AND CRACKED BLACK PEPPER (TO TASTE)

Make the lentils according to the directions that follow and place them in the fridge to chill.

Bring the large pot of salted water to a boil and add the Old Bay seasoning. The haricots verts, artichokes, potatoes, and eggs will all be cooked in this pot of water, which makes this seemingly complicated recipe much easier. Blanch the haricots verts in the water for 2 minutes, remove them from the boiling water, and place them into a bowl of ice water to stop the cooking process.

Trim the artichokes by peeling the tough outer part of the stem with a vegetable peeler, trimming off the top 1/3 of the leafy part, and then cutting artichoke in half lengthwise so a cross-section of the heart is exposed. Rub all cut parts of the artichoke with lemon to stop it from oxidizing.

Place the artichoke, lemon, and quartered new potatoes into the boiling water for 15 minutes. Remove the artichokes and potatoes to a bowl of ice water to stop the cooking process. The 'choke' should

continued on page 210

be easy to remove—just tug on the hairy-looking part just above the heart now that the artichokes are cooked through.

Lower the eggs into the boiling water for exactly 8 minutes and then remove to a bowl of ice water to stop the cooking process. (8 minutes will give you a custardy yolk, which we like.) Cook them for 10 minutes to achieve a solid center. Slice the eggs in quarters or slices.

Place a few leaves of butter lettuce in the center of a plate. Arrange the components any way you like. This can be a rustic salad or a composed plate. Drizzle the salad with Thyme and Tarragon Dressing and season with salt and pepper.

FRENCH GREEN LENTILS

- 1 1/4 CUPS VEGETABLE BROTH
- 1/2 CUP GREEN LENTILS
- 1 SPRIG THYME
- 1 BAY LEAF
- 1 TABLESPOON DIJON OR GRAINY MUSTARD

Into a medium pot over high heat, place the broth, lentils, thyme, bay leaf, and mustard. Bring to a boil, reduce the heat to a simmer, cover, and cook for 20 minutes. (Makes about 1 1/2 cups.)

THYME AND TARRAGON DRESSING

- 1 TABLESPOON DIJON MUSTARD
- 1 TABLESPOON LEMON JUICE
- 1 TEASPOON HONEY
- 4 TABLESPOONS OLIVE OIL
- 3 SPRIGS FRESH THYME
- 1/2 TEASPOON DRIED TARRAGON
- 1 TABLESPOON MINCED SHALLOT (RINSED)
- KOSHER SALT AND CRACKED BLACK PEPPER (TO TASTE)

Into a medium bowl, place the mustard, lemon juice, and honey. Slowly drizzle in the olive oil while whisking to emulsify the dressing. Stir in the thyme, tarragon, shallot, salt, and pepper. (Makes about 1/2 cup.)

CHICKPEA ENERGY SALAD

This is our re-set salad. No matter how you've been eating the rest of the day, it'll get you right back on track and give you a burst of afternoon energy so that you can get every last thing done. We sometimes eat plain chickpeas, just rinse 'em and go, but this recipe makes it a bit more civilized.

The cool thing about this salad is that you probably have all of the ingredients in your cupboard, and once you whip it up, you can have it on some couscous, in a wrap with sliced cucumbers, or on top of a bed of lettuce...or you could just eat it straight out of the bowl.

Serves 2.

- 1 TEASPOON CHAMPAGNE VINEGAR
- 1 TABLESPOON OLIVE OIL
- JUICE AND ZEST FROM 1 LEMON
- 1 CLOVE GARLIC (MINCED)

- 1/4 TEASPOON HONEY
- 1 15-OUNCE CAN CHICKPEAS (RINSED)
- 1 SHALLOT (MINCED, RINSED IN RUNNING WATER; ABOUT 1 TABLESPOON)
- 1 CUP GRAPE TOMATOES (HALVED)

- 2 TABLESPOONS MINCED PARSLEY
- KOSHER SALT AND CRACKED BLACK PEPPER (TO TASTE)

In a medium mixing bowl, whisk together the vinegar, olive oil, lemon juice, zest, garlic, and honey. Add chickpeas, shallot, tomatoes, and parsley. Season to taste with salt and pepper.

SPICY QUINOA AND BLACK LENTIL SALAD WITH AVOCADO VINAIGRETTE

Often, we want a salad that's more like a meal. There's no cheese and no bread in this (unless you opt to include a warmed tortilla on the side, which is an excellent idea), but the quinoa makes it pretty filling. The trick is the Avocado Vinaigrette, which you can't really place in the finished dish, but it's the component that adds so much flavor.

Serves 2.

- PICKLED RED ONION (RECIPE FOLLOWS)
- 1 CUP VEGETABLE BROTH (OR WATER)
- 1/2 CUP DRY BLACK LENTILS
- 1 1/2 CUPS PREPARED QUINOA (FOLLOW PACKAGE INSTRUCTIONS)

- 1 CUP DICED GREEN BELL PEPPER
- 1 CUP CORN (CUT AWAY FROM THE COB OR FROZEN)
- 1/4 TEASPOON CHIPOTLE PEPPER POWDER
- 1/2 TEASPOON CUMIN

- AVOCADO VINAIGRETTE (RECIPE FOLLOWS)
- KOSHER SALT AND CRACKED BLACK PEPPER (TO TASTE)
- GREENS, SLICED AVOCADO, CILANTRO LEAVES, OLIVE OIL (OPTIONAL) (TO GARNISH)

To prepare the lentils, bring 1 cup of broth or water to a boil in a medium pan and add 1/2 cup dry lentils. Cover and simmer for 20 minutes or until all liquid has been absorbed. Prepare the quinoa at the same time. Toast the corn kernels in a dry pan over medium-high heat until they start to brown. Allow the quinoa, lentils, and corn to cool. In a large mixing bowl, toss the onion (minus the pickling liquid), lentils, quinoa, pepper, corn, chipotle, and cumin together with the avocado vinaigrette. Add salt and pepper to taste. Serve on a bed of your favorite greens with avocado, cilantro, and a drizzle of olive oil.

PICKLED RED ONION

- 1 CUP DICED RED ONION (ABOUT 1 MEDIUM)
- 1/4 CUP WHITE VINEGAR
- 1/4 CUP WATER
- 1 TEASPOON SUGAR
- 1/2 TEASPOON KOSHER SALT

Add the onion, vinegar, water, sugar, and salt to a food storage container. Allow the mixture to sit in the fridge for at least 1 hour before straining and using as a garnish. (Makes 1 cup.)

AVOCADO VINAIGRETTE

- 1 CUP CILANTRO LEAVES
- 1 CLOVE GARLIC
- JUICE OF 1 LIME
- 1 SMALL CHILI PEPPER
  (LIKE A JALAPEÑO)
- 1/4 CUP WHITE WINE VINEGAR
- 1 TEASPOON HONEY
- KOSHER SALT AND CRACKED
  BLACK PEPPER (TO TASTE)
- 1 SMALL AVOCADO
- 1/4 CUP OLIVE OIL

Place the cilantro, garlic, lime juice, chili pepper, vinegar, honey, salt, pepper, and the flesh of the avocado into the work bowl of your food processor. Blend until smooth. While the processor is running, drizzle in the olive oil. Set aside until ready to use. (Makes 2 cups.)

GRILLED RADICCHIO SALAD WITH ORANGES & GOLDEN RAISINS

Radicchio is bitter. There is no way around it; it just is. We're not saying that's a bad thing. The deal with bitter greens—hey, if they're purple, could we still call them greens?—is that you have to do certain things to them so that you bring in some balance.

In this dish, we used sweet golden raisins and tangy orange segments in order to add some much-needed sweetness and acidity. Lightly grilling the radicchio also lends a subtle smoky flavor.

Serves 4.

- 1 LARGE HEAD OF RADICCHIO (ABOUT THE SIZE OF A GRAPEFRUIT, OR TWO SMALLER ONES)
- 1/4 CUP OLIVE OIL (DIVIDED)
- 1 TABLESPOON HONEY
- 1 TABLESPOON LEMON JUICE
- 1/4 CUP GOLDEN RAISINS
- 1/4 TEASPOON CRACKED BLACK PEPPER
- KOSHER SALT (TO TASTE)
- 1/4 CUP TOASTED, CHOPPED PECANS
- 1 MEDIUM ORANGE (SUPREMED)

Preheat your outdoor grill to high. (You may also use a cast-iron grill pan for this. Just preheat the grill pan over high heat, but remember that a cast-iron pan can get pretty smoky, so be sure to turn on the vent-a-hood first.)

Slice the large radicchio into quarters; leave the root end intact so that the leaves do not separate. Drizzle the cut radicchio with 1/8 cup of the olive oil. Grill the radicchio for about 20 to 30 seconds per side. You want grill marks and a smoky flavor, but you don't want to burn it. Remove the radicchio from the grill to a plate in order for it to rest while you make the dressing.

Place the honey and lemon juice in a medium mixing bowl. Whisk as you add the remaining 1/8 cup of olive oil. Add the raisins, pepper, and salt to taste.

To assemble the salad, place 1/4 of the grilled radicchio on each plate and press it with the palm of your hand. This will spread the leaves out just a bit for a nicer presentation. Divide the dressing, walnuts, and supremed orange slices among the salads. Add salt and pepper to taste.

THAI-STYLE PAPAYA SALAD

The first time we tried the real-deal green papaya salad at a Thai restaurant, we were struck by its strong, bright flavors. Our version, which uses a semi-ripe papaya for a sweeter spin on the classic, came about since we always see papayas at the store and wonder what we could do with them besides juice 'em. Ripe papayas seem to have more flavor and a better texture for this recipe. We realize it's not traditional, but that's kind of why we like it.

Serves 2.

- 1 MEDIUM FIRM, JUST-RIPE PAPAYA (2 1/2 CUPS SHREDDED)
- 1 HOT PEPPER (THAI BIRD CHILI OR SERRANO PEPPER)
- 1-INCH PIECE FRESH GINGER
- 1 CUP CILANTRO
- 1 CLOVE GARLIC

- 1 GREEN ONION (SLICED)
- JUICE OF 2 LIMES
- 1 TABLESPOON SOY SAUCE (LIKE BRAGG® LIQUID AMINOS)
- 1 TEASPOON SUGAR
- 1/2 CUP ROASTED PEANUTS (CHOPPED)

- 2 SPRIGS MINT (FOR GARNISH)
- SRIRACHA HOT SAUCE (TO TASTE)
- 10-12 LEAVES OF ROMAINE LETTUCE

Peel the papaya and shred the flesh using a serrated peeler or by slicing the flesh into thin matchsticks with a knife. You want to get all the papaya flesh while avoiding the large center cavity that's full of seeds. Set the shredded papaya aside and prepare the dressing.

In a food processor or using a mortar and pestle, blend the hot pepper, ginger, cilantro, and garlic. In a large bowl, whisk together the pepper, ginger, cilantro, and garlic mixture with the green onion, lime juice, soy sauce, sugar, and chopped peanuts. Add the shredded papaya and toss to coat.

Serve family-style garnished with mint sprigs and Sriracha with the romaine leaves on the side. To eat, fill a romaine leaf with the spicy papaya salad and top it with a mint leaf.

SWEET POTATO ALMONDINE

It turns out that if you put buttery toasted almonds on anything that's already even kind of good, you instantly make the dish beyond delicious. We love the balance of sweet and savory here, and it's a nice change from the usual mashed sweet potatoes or sweet potato fries.

Serves 4 as a side or 2 as a main dish.

- 2 MEDIUM SWEET POTATOES
- 1 TABLESPOON OLIVE OIL
- 1 TEASPOON APPLE CIDER VINEGAR
- KOSHER SALT AND CRACKED BLACK PEPPER (TO TASTE)
- 2 TABLESPOONS UNSALTED BUTTER
- 1 CUP SLICED ALMONDS
- 1 PEELED SHALLOT (THINLY SLICED)
- 1/4 CUP PARSLEY LEAVES (TO GARNISH)
- HALF OF A LEMON

Preheat your outdoor grill to high. Using a sharp knife or mandoline, slice the sweet potatoes into 1/4-inch slices. In a large bowl, toss the sweet potato slices with the olive oil and the vinegar. Add salt and pepper to taste. Grill the slices of sweet potato for 5 minutes per side or until well-marked by the grill grates. Remove and cover.

In a large frying pan over medium heat, melt the butter and add the almonds. Cook until toasted and fragrant. Remove from the heat and set aside.

Assemble the dish by shingling the sweet potatoes on a large platter and topping them with the buttery almonds. Garnish with shallot and parsley. Squeeze lemon over the dish and season with salt and pepper to taste.

MICHAEL'S TRUFFLED CORN PUDDING

When our good friend Michael made this amazing corn pudding for us one summer, we just had to snag his recipe. We topped our pudding with cute little chanterelle mushrooms sautéed in butter and thyme, but this dish is so versatile you could serve it with almost anything.

Serves 4.

- 5 EARS OF CORN
- ¼ CUP 2% MILK
- ¼ CUP HALF-AND-HALF
- 1 TEASPOON KOSHER SALT
- 2 LARGE EGGS (DIVIDED)
- 1 EGG YOLK

- 1 TABLESPOON UNSALTED BUTTER (MELTED)
- 1 TABLESPOON TRUFFLE BUTTER (MELTED)
- 2 TABLESPOONS ALL-PURPOSE FLOUR

- 2 TABLESPOONS CORN MEAL OR GRITS
- ¼ CUP ROMANO CHEESE
- 1/8 TEASPOON SMOKED PAPRIKA

Preheat your oven to 400 degrees. Cut the corn off the cob. In the bowl with the corn, scrape the cut cobs with a spoon; that will release the corn 'milk' and pulp still remaining in the cob. In a separate bowl, mix the milk, half and half, salt, eggs, egg yolk, and melted butters. (Note: If you don't have truffle butter, just substitute another tablespoon of unsalted butter.) Whisk it all together. Add the flour and grits and whisk again. Add the corn mixture and stir to combine. Pour into a shallow, buttered baking dish. Sprinkle with cheese and paprika. Bake for 25 minutes or until golden brown. Once cooked, let it sit for 10 minutes to settle.

BAKED ARANCINI WITH SMOKED PROVOLONE

Arancini's like a rounded, fancier version of a breaded cheese stick—seriously, how could you go wrong with that? Usually fried, arancini is just as good when it's baked. Once we tried it this way, we really loved it.

Serves 4.

- 1 CUP ARBORIO OR SUSHI RICE
- 1 TEASPOON ITALIAN SEASONING
- 1/4 TEASPOON GARLIC POWDER
- 1/4 TEASPOON RED PEPPER FLAKES
- CRACKED BLACK PEPPER (TO TASTE)

- ZEST OF 1 LEMON
- 1/4 CUP FLAT-LEAF PARSLEY (MINCED)
- 3 CUPS WARM VEGETABLE BROTH
- 2 LARGE EGGS
- 2 TABLESPOONS WATER
- 1 1/4 CUPS PANKO BREAD CRUMBS (DIVIDED)

- 3 OUNCES SMOKED PROVOLONE CHEESE (CUT INTO 1/2-INCH CUBES)
- 8 TEASPOONS OLIVE OIL
- TOMATO SAUCE (TO SERVE)
- PARMESAN CHEESE (TO GARNISH)

Into a medium pot over medium heat, add the rice, Italian seasoning, garlic powder, red pepper flakes, black pepper, lemon zest, parsley, and 1 cup of the broth. Stir to incorporate. Cook, uncovered, for 6 to 8 minutes; stir occasionally to make sure the bottom doesn't scorch. Add another cup of broth, stir, and cook another 6 to 8 minutes. Finally, add the last of the broth and stir and cook another 6 to 8 minutes or until the rice is tender and has absorbed most of the liquid. Cover and allow mixture to cool completely.

Preheat your oven to 350 degrees and line a baking sheet with parchment. Once the rice mixture has cooled, add one beaten egg and 1/4 cup of the panko bread crumbs. Stir to incorporate. Set up two bowls: one with the remaining egg beaten with 2 tablespoons of water, and the other with the remaining cup of panko bread crumbs. Using a 1/4-cup ice cream scoop, scoop out a portion of the rice mixture, place a cube of cheese into the middle, and then roll it into a round ball completely enclosing the cheese. Dip the ball into the egg, roll it in the panko to coat, and place it onto the parchment-lined baking sheet. (You will make 8 arancini.) Drizzle each ball with about 1 teaspoon of olive oil and bake for 30 minutes or until golden brown. Serve with tomato sauce and garnish with grated Parmesan.

DESSERTS

· ·

FROZEN PEANUT BUTTER BANANA PIE

This vegan, gluten-free pie is great for summer birthday celebrations and backyard grilling parties. The frozen and blended bananas really end up tasting a lot like ice cream! With dates used as the sweetener and lots of nutritious ingredients included, this is a great alternative to a store-bought ice cream cake.

Serves 8.

- 5 RIPE BANANAS
- 1 CUP ROASTED AND SALTED PEANUTS
- 1/2 CUP PEANUT BUTTER
- 5 DRIED DATES (PITTED)
- 1 TABLESPOON COCOA POWDER
- 1/2 CUP UNSWEETENED ALMOND MILK
- 1/2 TEASPOON MALDON® SEA SALT FLAKES
- CHOCOLATE SYRUP (TO GARNISH)

Peel the bananas and freeze them for at least 3 hours. Into the work bowl of your food processor, place the peanuts and pulse until finely chopped. Into the bottom of a springform pan, spread the finely chopped peanuts in an even layer.

Slice the frozen bananas into chunks. Into the work bowl of the same food processor, place the bananas, peanut butter, dates, cocoa powder, almond milk, and salt. Blend until smooth. Gently pour mixture into the springform pan so as not to disturb the layer of peanuts on the bottom. Smooth the mixture with a rubber spatula by pushing the mixture to the edges. Place the springform pan in the freezer for at least an hour. For the best consistency, remove the pie from the freezer 10 minutes before serving so it softens a bit. Slice and drizzle with chocolate syrup.

MIXED BERRY CRISP FOR A CROWD

Whenever you're planning have everyone over for a summer get-together, know that this recipe serves at least 10 folks (if that's too many, just halve it) and that it's really easy to throw together the morning of the party. It's got some good nutritional elements, and it's great with ice cream or Greek yogurt on top or even just by itself.

Serves 10.

- 10 CUPS FROZEN BERRIES (ANY COMBINATION STRAWBERRIES, BLUEBERRIES, BLACKBERRIES, RASPBERRIES)
- 1 CUP HONEY
- 1 1/2 TEASPOONS MALDON® SEA SALT FLAKES (DIVIDED)

- JUICE FROM 1 LEMON
- 1 TABLESPOON OLIVE OIL
- 2 CUPS OATS
- 1 CUP PECANS (FINELY CHOPPED)
- 1 CUP SPROUTED WHEAT FLOUR
- 1 CUP LIGHT BROWN SUGAR

- 2 TABLESPOONS SPICES (ANY COMBINATION OF CINNAMON, NUTMEG, ALLSPICE, GINGER, AND CLOVE)
- 2/3 CUP COCONUT OIL
- ICE CREAM OR GREEK YOGURT (OPTIONAL, FOR TOPPING)

Preheat your oven to 350 degrees. Microwave the frozen berries for one minute. Drizzle the honey over the berries and stir it in so that it coats them. Sprinkle the 1/2 teaspoon salt over them and add the lemon juice and stir again to combine. Brush olive oil on the bottom and sides of your baking dish(es); we often use two for this recipe. Spread out the fruit in about a one-inch layer and bake it by itself for 10-15 minutes while you make the topping.

In a medium-sized bowl, stir together the oats, pecans, flour, light brown sugar, 1 teaspoon salt, and spices. Drizzle in the coconut oil and mix well. Take the berry mixture out of the oven and spread the topping over it evenly. (You won't have a thick layer; it's perfectly fine for some fruit to peek through the topping.)

Bake for 1 hour or until the topping is golden brown and the fruit has cooked down to a jam-like consistency. Cool before serving and top with ice cream or Greek yogurt.

ENERGY COOKIES

We love having these cookies on hand as an afternoon snack option because, well, they taste better than the usual granola bar from a box. With the combo of nuts, dried fruit, oats, coconut, and honey, they offer some solid nutrition, and they're great with a big glass of unsweetened vanilla almond milk.

Makes 24 cookies.

- 1 CUP ROLLED OATS
- 3/4 CUP ALMOND FLOUR
- 1 TEASPOON BAKING POWDER
- 2 TEASPOONS MALDON® SEA SALT FLAKES
- 1 1/2 TEASPOONS CINNAMON
- 1 TEASPOON GROUND GINGER
- 1/2 TEASPOON NUTMEG
- 1/2 CUP HONEY
- 1/2 CUP COCONUT OIL (MELTED)
- 2 LARGE EGGS (BEATEN)
- 2 TEASPOONS VANILLA
- 3/4 CUP RAISINS (A MIX OF GOLDEN AND THOMPSON)
- 1/3 CUP DRIED CRANBERRIES
- 2 TABLESPOONS RUM
- 1 CUP GRATED DRIED COCONUT
- 2 TABLESPOONS CRYSTALLIZED GINGER (FINELY DICED)
- 1 CUP WALNUTS

Preheat your oven to 350 degrees. Stir together the oats, almond flour, baking powder, sea salt flakes, cinnamon, ginger, and nutmeg and set aside. Whisk together the honey, coconut oil, eggs, and vanilla and set aside. Microwave the raisins, cranberries, and rum for one minute. Let the mixture cool for a few minutes, microwave it for one more minute, and set aside.

Combine the wet and dry ingredients and then add the fruit and rum mixture, coconut, ginger, and walnuts. Shape into flat cookies about two to three inches in diameter and place on a parchment-lined baking sheet. Bake for 10-15 minutes until the edges are lightly browned.

SPARKLING, SPICY FRUIT

There's nothing more refreshing or fun to eat than this layered fruit cup! You sip it and also crunch it. It's a spicy soda and a refreshing dessert rolled into one. It's got tropical fruit, honey-roasted peanuts, and dates, and it's topped off with a honey, raspberry, and cayenne syrup.

We've modeled it after the Mexican tradition of eating fruit with lime and chili pepper, but the best version in Memphis is at a place called Las Jarochos on Summer Avenue. Our own version of their 'Tornado' uses local honey and raspberries to mimic the traditional chamoy, a sweet and spicy Mexican condiment used mainly as a dip for fruit.

Serves 2 to 4.

- 1 PERSONAL-SIZED, SEEDLESS WATERMELON (CUBED, RIND DISCARDED)
- 1 SMALL JICAMA (PEELED, CUBED)
- 2 LARGE MANGOES (PEELED, CUBED)
- 1 MEDIUM PINEAPPLE (PEELED, CORED, CUBED)
- 1 MEDIUM ENGLISH CUCUMBER (CUBED)
- 1/4 TEASPOON KOSHER SALT
- 4-8 DRIED MEDJOOL DATES
- 1 CUP HONEY-ROASTED PEANUTS
- SPICY RASPBERRY-HONEY SYRUP (RECIPE FOLLOWS)
- 2 12-OUNCE CANS SPARKLING WATER
- 6 STRAWBERRIES

Once all the fruit is cut and chilled, sprinkle the fruit cubes with Kosher salt. Layer the cubed watermelon, jicama, mango, pineapple, and cucumber into 2 quart jars or 4 pint jars. Thread two or three dates onto each drinking straw and place a straw in each jar. Top each jar with 1/4 cup of honey-roasted peanuts.

Top with a generous spoonful or two of Spicy Raspberry-Honey Syrup. Top it all off with sparkling water and garnish the rim with strawberries.

NOTE: Special equipment needed: 4 metal drinking straws

....

SPICY RASPBERRY-HONEY SYRUP

- 1/2 CUP LIME JUICE (FROM 4 TO 5 MEDIUM LIMES)
- 1/2 CUP HONEY
- 1/4 TEASPOON CAYENNE
- 1/4 TEASPOON MALDON® SEA SALT FLAKES
- 1/2 CUP RASPBERRIES

Into the work bowl of your food processor, place the lime juice, honey, cayenne, salt, and raspberries. Blend until smooth. Set aside until ready to use. (Makes 1 1/4 cups.)

BLUEBERRY AND CREAM SNOW CONES

This is actually an easy granita, but isn't it more fun to just go ahead and call it a snow cone? Fresh, in-season blueberries and local honey make it, in our minds, the best snow cone ever. We add orange flower water to enhance the strong floral note that fresh summer blueberries possess.

Serves 6.

- 2 PINTS FRESH BLUEBERRIES
- 2 CUPS WATER
- 1/2 CUP SUGAR
- JUICE OF 1 LEMON

- 1/4 TEASPOON ORANGE FLOWER WATER
- 2 TABLESPOONS HONEY

- HALF AND HALF (TO GARNISH)

In a medium pan over medium heat, cook the blueberries, water, sugar, and lemon juice for 10 minutes in order to soften the berries. Run the mixture through a food mill or blend it in a food processor and strain it using a fine mesh strainer to remove the blueberry pulp. Stir in the orange flower water and the honey. Set aside and allow the mixture to cool.

Pour mixture into a 9 x 13-inch freezer-proof casserole dish and place the dish into the freezer. After one hour, stir the mixture; use a fork to break up any lumps and return it to the freezer. After another hour, use a fork to scrape the surface of the ice. Stir it, pack it back down, and return it to the freezer. After one additional hour of freezing time, it will be ready to serve.

To serve, scrape the surface of the ice with the tines of a fork. This will create what looks like purple snow. Using an ice cream scoop, place two scoops in each cup and top each serving with 1 1/2 teaspoons of half and half.

AVOCADO-WALNUT BROWNIES

No-butter, no-oil brownies? Seriously? With avocado instead of butter...okay, wow! A little while ago, this secret brownie ingredient developed into quite a thing online amongst the vegans and the Paleo loyalists and general health-conscious folks. If you're deterred in the slightest, know that surprisingly enough, you won't really taste the avocado.

Serves 8.

- 1 RIPE AVOCADO (MASHED)
- 2/3 CUP SUGAR
- 3 TABLESPOONS COCOA POWDER
- 3 OUNCES OF A DARK CHOCOLATE BAR

- 1/8 CUP MILK
- 2 LARGE EGGS
- 1/4 CUP ALL-PURPOSE FLOUR
- 1 TEASPOON ESPRESSO POWDER

- 1/4 TEASPOON BAKING SODA
- 1/2 TEASPOON MALDON® SEA SALT FLAKES
- 1 TEASPOON VANILLA
- 1/2 CUP CHOPPED WALNUTS

Preheat your oven to 350 degrees. In your stand mixer, mix the avocado, sugar, and cocoa powder. Melt the chocolate and milk in the microwave for 30 seconds, stir, and melt for another 30 seconds. Stir again and add the chocolate mixture to the stand mixer ingredients. Mix until combined. Add the eggs, flour, espresso, baking soda, salt, and vanilla and mix until combined. Spread batter into a 5 x 8-inch pan lined with parchment paper. Top with the chopped walnuts. Bake for 20 minutes. Let the pan of brownies cool for 30 minutes and then lift the brownies out using the edges of the paper. Store them in a container in the fridge.

RICE KHEER

We often try our best to re-create some of our favorite Indian dishes. Here we have a classic dessert, Rice Kheer, simply a mix of raisins, rice, cashews, and noodles or tapioca in green cardamom-scented, sweetened milk. It's best served warm after a dinner of curry and dosas.

Serves 4.

- 3 CUPS WHOLE MILK
- 1/2 CUP SUGAR
- 1 TABLESPOON WHOLE GREEN CARDAMOM PODS (CRUSHED)
- 1/4 TEASPOON MALDON® SEA SALT FLAKES
- 1 TABLESPOON UNSALTED BUTTER
- 1/2 CUP DRY RICE VERMICELLI (BROKEN INTO SMALL PIECES)
- 1/2 CUP ROASTED, UNSALTED CASHEWS (CHOPPED)
- 1/2 CUP COOKED AND COOLED BASMATI RICE
- 1/4 CUP THOMPSON RAISINS
- 1/4 CUP GOLDEN RAISINS

Place the milk, sugar, salt, and cardamom in a cold pot. Slowly raise the temperature under the pot, and stir constantly in order to prevent scorching. Once the mixture reaches a boil, strain through a fine mesh strainer and set aside and keep warm.

Melt the butter in a medium skillet over medium heat. Sauté the vermicelli and cashews in the butter until they're fragrant and lightly browned. Place equal amounts of the milk mixture, noodle mixture, rice, and raisins in four small bowls. After 5 minutes, the noodles will be soft, and the Rice Kheer will be ready to be served warm.

BOURBON, ORANGE, AND DARK CHOCOLATE SOUFFLÉ

One sweet we both love is candied orange slices dipped in dark chocolate. Our local candy store, Dinstuhl's in Memphis, does these right; when we stop in to check out their Easter, Halloween, and Christmas displays, we always grab some chocolate-dipped orange slices to go. This chocolate and orange soufflé mimics their flavor and features an extra note of bourbon.

Serves 4.

- 5 EGGS (SEPARATED, ONE YOLK DISCARDED)
- 1/4 CUP SUGAR
- 1 70% CHOCOLATE BAR (3.5 OUNCES, CHOPPED)
- 1 TABLESPOON BOURBON

- ZEST FROM 1 ORANGE (ABOUT ONE TABLESPOON)
- 1 TEASPOON VANILLA
- 1/4 TEASPOON MALDON® SEA SALT FLAKES
- 1/4 CUP HALF-AND-HALF

- 1/4 TEASPOON CREAM OF TARTAR
- 1 TEASPOON POWDERED SUGAR (TO GARNISH)
- 2 ORANGES (PEELED, SUPREMED)

Preheat your oven to 375 degrees. Fill a medium saucepan halfway with water and place over high heat. Place the four egg yolks into a medium-sized metal bowl along with the sugar, chopped chocolate, bourbon, orange zest, vanilla, salt, and half-and-half. Once the water in the saucepan begins to boil, place the bowl with the yolk and chocolate mixture over the water so that the bowl doesn't touch the water. Whisk until all of the chocolate has melted. Remove the bowl from the heat and set it aside to cool.

Place the 5 cold egg whites in another medium bowl along with the cream of tartar. Whisk vigorously for four to five minutes or until the whites form soft peaks. (Soft peaks look like this: pick some of the whites up with the end of the whisk, and it forms peaks that fold over. They'll look kind of like a Santa hat!)

Take half of the whisked egg whites and add them to the cooled chocolate mixture. Mix that thoroughly with a whisk. Using a rubber spatula, carefully fold the remaining whites into the mixture while retaining as much of the fluffiness as possible. Divide the mixture between the four ramekins. Bake for 12-15 minutes or until the top is craggy. Garnish with powdered sugar and orange segments.

NOTE: Special equipment: four small one-inch by five-inch ramekins

PINE NUT COOKIES

We've decided that hoarding pine nuts and using them sparingly is just too stingy. You need to use a bunch of them to coat these Italian cookies, which are often called Pignoli Amaretti, but you can make up for the expense by food processing your own almond paste for them instead of relying on store-bought. These are not too sweet and have a toasted, rich, marzipan-like flavor and an airy, chewy, and smooth texture.

Makes 20 cookies.

- 1 CUP SLICED ALMONDS
- 1/2 CUP POWDERED SUGAR
- 1/2 CUP SUGAR
- 1/2 TEASPOON VANILLA
- 1 EGG
- 1/4 TEASPOON MALDON® SEA SALT FLAKES
- 1/4 TEASPOON BAKING POWDER
- 1/2 CUP ALL-PURPOSE FLOUR
- 1 1/2 CUPS PINE NUTS

Preheat your oven to 350 degrees. Blend the almonds in the food processor for two minutes until a paste forms; add a little water a teaspoon at a time if moisture is needed for the paste to come together. Add the two sugars and vanilla and pulse. Add the egg and pulse. Combine the sea salt, baking powder, and all-purpose flour. Add this mixture to the food processor with the other ingredients and pulse again until just mixed.

Spread the pine nuts in a single layer on a plate. Using a small scoop, place dough onto the pine nuts and press it into the cookie to coat one side. Place the cookies on a parchment-lined baking sheet. Bake for 10 minutes or until golden brown. Use a spatula to place cookies on a cooling rack for a few minutes before serving.

SPICED PECAN GRANOLA

- 2 TABLESPOONS SORGHUM
- 2 1/2 TABLESPOONS OLIVE OIL
- 1 TABLESPOON LIGHT BROWN SUGAR
- 1 TEASPOON VANILLA
- 1/2 TEASPOON CINNAMON
- 1/4 TEASPOON GINGER
- PINCH OF NUTMEG
- 1/2 TEASPOON MALDON® SEA SALT FLAKES
- 3/4 CUP ROLLED OATS
- 3/4 CUP PECANS (ROUGHLY CHOPPED)

Preheat your oven to 350 degrees. In a medium bowl, whisk the sorghum, oil, sugar, vanilla, cinnamon, ginger, nutmeg, and salt until well-incorporated. Pour in the oats and pecans and mix until well-coated. Spread the granola mixture into a thin layer on a parchment-lined baking sheet. Bake on your oven's lower rack for 15 minutes total, but take out the granola and turn the baking sheet and stir it up halfway through the baking time. Place the granola on a plate to cool. (Makes about 1 1/2 cups.)

WHITE-WINE-POACHED PEARS WITH SPICED PECAN GRANOLA AND HONEY-LEMON RICOTTA

Arguably, one of the best parts of fall is the fruit, and we celebrate it by poaching fresh pears in wine and topping that with honey-lemon ricotta and crunchy, almost savory granola. It's a dessert that's a bit more savory than sweet, and we love thinking of different ways to use the syrup that forms once the poaching liquid is reduced.

Serves 8.

- 4 PEARS (PEELED, HALVED, AND CORED)
- 1 BOTTLE WHITE WINE
- 1/3 CUP HONEY
- 8 DRIED JUNIPER BERRIES
- 2 CINNAMON STICKS
- 1 BAY LEAF
- 1-INCH PIECE FRESH GINGER (SLICED)
- PINCH OF MALDON® SEA SALT FLAKES
- SPICED PECAN GRANOLA (RECIPE ON PREVIOUS PAGE)
- HONEY-LEMON RICOTTA (RECIPE FOLLOWS)

Place the pear halves cut-side-down into a 12-inch stainless steel frying pan. Pour in the bottle of wine and the honey. Add the juniper, cinnamon, bay leaf, ginger, and salt. Place the frying pan on the stovetop over medium heat and allow the liquid to reduce. Cook for 45 minutes; be sure to flip the pears halfway through this cooking time. When the liquid is syrupy and coats the back of a spoon, remove the pan from the heat. Place the pear halves on a serving dish and strain the wine syrup. Discard the solid ingredients and reserve the syrup for serving.

To serve, place a heaping tablespoon of Honey-Lemon Ricotta into the cored section of each pear. Add the Spiced Pecan Granola on top. Drizzle with the wine syrup.

HONEY-LEMON RICOTTA

- 1 CUP WHOLE MILK RICOTTA CHEESE
- 2 TABLESPOONS HONEY
- 1 TEASPOON VANILLA
- ZEST OF 1 LEMON
- PINCH OF MALDON® SEA SALT FLAKES

In a medium bowl, whisk the ricotta, honey, vanilla, lemon zest, and salt until well-incorporated. Set aside until ready to serve. (Makes about 1 cup.)

SPICY BANANA AND ALMOND DATE BITES

Sometimes we need a snack that we can feel great about enjoying, one that tricks us into eating whole ingredients but doesn't taste completely boring. These vegan, cayenne-spiked energy bites require no cooking; consider them modern trail mix!

Makes 12 bites.

- 1/2 CUP DRIED BANANA CHIPS
- 1/2 CUP SLICED ALMONDS (TOASTED) PLUS 1 TABLESPOON (FOR GARNISH)
- 1 HEAPING CUP PITTED DATES (ABOUT 25)
- 1/2 TEASPOON CAYENNE
- 1/4 TEASPOON CINNAMON
- 1/2 TEASPOON MALDON® SEA SALT FLAKES

Place the banana chips in the food processor and pulse until they form a chunky powder. Add 1/2 cup almonds and the dates and blend until everything's broken down into small granules. Add the cayenne, cinnamon, and salt and pulse until combined. Form the mixture into 1-inch orbs using your hands; you will make about 12 bites. Add an almond slice or two on top to garnish.

SAUCES & EXTRAS

· ·

SPICY SRIRACHA PEANUT SAUCE

- 2 TABLESPOONS PEANUT BUTTER
- 2 TABLESPOONS MIRIN
- 2 TABLESPOONS SOY SAUCE
  (LIKE BRAGG® LIQUID AMINOS)
- 2 TABLESPOONS SRIRACHA HOT SAUCE
- 1 CLOVE GARLIC

Using an immersion blender or food processor, blend the peanut butter, mirin, soy sauce, Sriracha, and garlic until smooth. Add enough water to get a pourable but still thick consistency. (Makes about 1/2 cups.)

THE CHUBBY VEGETARIAN'S SIGNATURE MEMPHIS DRY RUB

- 2 PARTS CHIPOTLE CHILI POWDER
- 2 PARTS SWEET PAPRIKA
- 2 PARTS SMOKED PAPRIKA
- 2 PARTS GRANULATED GARLIC
- 2 PARTS KOSHER SALT
- 2 PARTS CRACKED BLACK PEPPER
- 2 PARTS CUMIN
- 2 PARTS DRIED THYME
- 2 PARTS DRIED OREGANO
- 1 PART CINNAMON
- 1 PART GROUND GINGER
- 1 PART BROWN SUGAR
- 1 PART POWDERED, DRIED PORCINI
  MUSHROOMS

You will measure all ingredients by volume. Mix all ingredients in a large food storage bag until all are equally distributed. Make as little or as much as you like based on this ratio.

NOTE: Dried porcini mushrooms can be found at almost any specialty grocery, often in the bulk bin area. Turn the dried mushrooms into a powder by placing them in a coffee grinder or food processor and pulsing until no large bits remain.

HICKORY SMOKED HOT SAUCE

We use cowhorn peppers to create this particular hot sauce, but you could use any combination of your favorite hot peppers for this. Keep in mind that the hotter the pepper, the hotter the sauce, so choose according to your own tolerance. While it's plenty spicy, this sauce is all about flavor, not just heat. The smoke and salt add a ton of great flavor to greens, tacos, cornbread, sandwiches, and soups.

- 8 CUPS FRESH CHILI PEPPERS (DE-STEMMED)
- 1 LARGE HEAD GARLIC (BROKEN INTO CLOVES)
- 2 TABLESPOONS KOSHER OR PICKLING SALT
- 1 1/2 CUPS WHITE VINEGAR
- 1/4 TEASPOON XANTHAN GUM (OPTIONAL)

Smoke the chili peppers for 6 minutes. Add 1/4 of the peppers to the work bowl of your food processor. Process until very finely chopped and then place into a large, non-reactive ceramic bowl. Repeat with the rest of the peppers and the garlic. Add the salt to the mix, stir with a rubber spatula, and pack the mixture into a 1-quart glass jar. The mixture should just about fill the jar. With the top loosely set, leave the glass jar with the pepper mixture out on the counter for 24 hours to ferment. (If the jar is particularly full, place a plate topped with a dishtowel underneath it in case it bubbles over.)

Place the contents of the jar back into a large, non-reactive bowl, mix in the vinegar, cover, and allow it to sit out on the countertop for an additional 24 hours to develop flavor. After that, use a fine mesh strainer to strain the mixture, pressing out all of the liquid until all that's left in the strainer is dry pulp. At this point, place the strained mixture into a blender and add the xanthan gum. Run the blender continuously for 1 minute to make sure the xanthan gum is blended in well; this step will keep your hot sauce from separating in the bottle. (Makes about a quart, depending on how juicy the peppers are.)

VEGETARIAN FISH SAUCE

Fish sauce is one of those ingredients that everyone seems to be using these days. You see it in everything from cuisine to cocktails. The world has gone fish sauce crazy! So, what is it? It's made of tiny fish that are heavily salted and fermented in huge barrels for a year or more. The result is a salty, bacon-y, parmesan-esque sauce that adds a ton of umami flavor to anything it touches.

Our fish-less fish sauce works anywhere you'd normally use the fishy stuff, and from all accounts, it tastes pretty close to the real deal. Keep some around to use in stir-fry, Thai curries, kimchi, and salad dressings. It also makes a great addition to stocks and soups that need a little umami bump.

- 1 QUART WATER
- 1 TABLESPOON GRANULATED GARLIC
- 1 TEASPOON RED PEPPER FLAKES
- 1.76-OUNCE PACKAGE KOMBU (RINSED BRIEFLY UNDER COLD WATER)
- 1 1/4 CUPS DRIED SHIITAKE MUSHROOMS
- 1/2 CUP SOY SAUCE (LIKE BRAGG® LIQUID AMINOS)

- 1 TABLESPOON SUGAR
- 2 TEASPOONS KOSHER SALT
- 1 TABLESPOON PEPPERCORNS
- 1 TEASPOON GROUND GINGER
- 2 TABLESPOONS RICE VINEGAR
- JUICE OF 1 LEMON
- JUICE OF 1 LIME

In a medium pot over hight heat, bring the water, garlic, red pepper flakes, kombu, shiitake, soy sauce, sugar, salt, peppercorns, ginger, vinegar, lemon juice, and lime juice up to a boil, cover, and reduce to a simmer. Allow the mixture to simmer for 25 to 30 minutes, strain, and return liquid to the pot. Bring back to a boil and reduce the mixture to 1 pint. Allow the mixture to cool and store in an airtight container in the fridge for up to 6 weeks. (Makes about 1 pint.)

SMOKY SRIRACHA

Sriracha, that now-ubiquitous spicy red sauce, is one of our all-time favorite things. We use it in our spicy peanut sauce, on grilled corn, and in soups, stews, and curries. Really, we just drizzle it on anything that needs a little flavor boost—even breakfast! So why is this stuff so good? It hits hard on many fronts: it's salty, spicy, a little acidic, and a little sweet. In other words, it's nearly perfect. So, we messed with it, of course.

Rather than add sugar, we roasted red jalapeños to bring out their natural sweetness. This process also provides a nice bit of smokiness, which really ups the ante by adding an additional note to traditional Sriracha sauce's symphony of flavor.

This sauce is really simple to make, and the ingredients aren't that hard to find. If red jalapeños aren't available—we usually find them at the Asian market in Memphis—you can make a sauce that's just as delicious using green ones. The xanthan gum is totally optional. All it does it keep the sauce from separating in the fridge. If you decide not to add it, just stir up the Sriracha before each use.

- 8 CUPS RED JALAPEÑO PEPPERS
- 1/2 CUP PEELED GARLIC CLOVES
- 1/2 CUP UNSEASONED RICE VINEGAR

- 1 TABLESPOON KOSHER SALT
- 1/4 TEASPOON XANTHAN GUM (OPTIONAL)

Over a fire or under your oven's broiler, roast the red jalapeños until blackened, just as you would do if you were roasting a red bell pepper. Place the roasted red jalapeños and the raw garlic cloves into a covered container and allow them to cool. Once it's all cool enough to handle, use a pair of kitchen shears to trim off the stems and discard them. Into your blender or food processor, place the trimmed jalapeños (blackened skin and all!), garlic, vinegar, salt, and xanthan gum and blend until smooth. Store it in an airtight container in the fridge. (Makes 2 cups.)

VEGETARIAN KIMCHI

We got a hot tip about how to make delicious kimchi from Sue Reyna, the owner of Kwik Check, a great sandwich shop on Madison Avenue in Memphis. She told us that the reason their kimchi is so good is that they use a ground-up Korean pear in each batch as a sweet element to balance out the bitterness of the cabbage. Brilliant! But where in the heck were we going to find a Korean pear? Sue disappeared into the kitchen and emerged with a larger-than-softball-sized fruit that had a golden skin. She was willing to let us have it since we wanted to try making our own kimchi.

There was one more hurdle to conquer before we could make our own kimchi: we needed some Korean red chili powder. We found some at an Asian market; the bright red powder was in a huge bag and cost $10. In the end, we were really glad that we shelled out for it because it made our kimchi taste pretty authentic.

At home, we sliced into the fruit to see what it tasted like before we ground it down with the chili paste. The texture was a cross between a crunchy apple and a Bartlett pear, and the flavor was similar to honeysuckle on a summer's day. Use this kimchi on rice, in soups, folded into a quesadilla, or in our Kimchi and Peanut Dumplings (page 62).

- 1 LARGE HEAD OF NAPA CABBAGE
- 1/4 CUP KOSHER OR PICKLING SALT
- 2-TO-3-INCH PIECE FRESH GINGER
- 1 SMALL BULB GARLIC (ABOUT 10 CLOVES, PEELED)
- 1 LARGE KOREAN PEAR (PEELED, CUT AWAY FROM CORE)
- 1/2 CUP KOREAN RED CHILI POWDER
- 1/4 CUP VEGETARIAN FISH SAUCE (RECIPE ON PAGE 254)
- 2 TABLESPOONS SUGAR
- 1 CUP DAIKON RADISH (SHREDDED USING A JULIENNE PEELER)
- 1 CUP CARROT (SHREDDED USING A JULIENNE PEELER)
- SRIRACHA HOT SAUCE (TO TASTE)

Wash the cabbage and chop into 1-inch pieces. Place the cabbage into a large bowl and toss it with the salt. Allow the mixture to sit unrefrigerated for at least an hour and a half.

While you're waiting, make the chili paste. Place the ginger, garlic, pear, chili powder, Vegetarian Fish Sauce, and sugar into a food processor. Blend until smooth; you may need to add a few tablespoons of water to get it going. Set the mixture aside.

Now fill the large bowl with the cabbage in it full of cold water and rinse the salt off of the cabbage. Do this twice. Using your hands, squeeze as much moisture out of the cabbage as you can. In a large bowl, toss the cabbage together with the garlic, ginger, and chili paste. Add the radish and carots and toss until every component is throughly coated with the red paste. Taste for seasoning and add salt and Sriracha if needed. It should be about as salty as a dill pickle and about as spicy as you can handle.

Place the kimchi into 2 quart jars by pushing the ingredients and packing them down tightly so that the liquid rests on the top. Leave about an inch of space at the top of the jar. Add a few tablespoons of water to the top if needed in order to submerge cabbage. You may enjoy the kimchi just as it is or ferment it for a more authentic taste.

To ferment the kimchi, loosely screw the tops on the jars and place jars on the countertop for 3 to 4 days. During this time, you will definitely notice some bubbling. This is a natural process called lactic fermentation, a method of food preservation used way before refrigeration, and it results in a lemony flavor almost like lemon-lime soda. (You may want to place the jars on plates to prevent overflow onto the countertop.) At the end of the fermentation period, screw the lids on the jars and place them in the fridge. Kimchi will last 6 weeks as long as the cabbage stays below the liquid level. (Makes about 2 quarts.)

WHOLE WHEAT NAAN

The best thing about going to your favorite Indian restaurant is the naan, that warm, garlicky bread. What could be better? Parts of the bread are crisp, other parts are chewy, there is the perfect amount of char, and it's always fresh out of the tandoori oven.

Here's a great version of this Indian staple that you can make at home without investing in a special oven. The whole wheat pastry flour adds a bit of nuttiness, and the yogurt lends richness to the dough.

- 1/2 CUP ALL-PURPOSE FLOUR
- 1/2 CUP WHOLE WHEAT PASTRY FLOUR
- 1/4 TEASPOON RAPID-RISE YEAST
- 1/4 TEASPOON KOSHER SALT
- 3/4 TO 1 CUP 2% GREEK YOGURT

- GARLIC BUTTER (1 TABLESPOON MELTED BUTTER WITH 1 LARGE CLOVE MINCED GARLIC)
- 1/4 CUP CHOPPED FLAT-LEAF PARSLEY
- MALDON® SEA SALT FLAKES (TO TASTE)

Place the dry ingredients into the food processor with the dough blade already in place. Turn the processor on and spoon in the yogurt until the dough clumps into a ball and rolls around the bowl. (You may not use the entire cup of yogurt.) Stop the processor, grab the dough, cut it in half, and then cut each half in half again to form four pieces. Roll each piece into a ball. Cover dough with a large bowl, and allow it to rise for 30 minutes.

Place a pizza stone on the upper-middle rack of the oven. Turn the broiler on medium-high and preheat for 20 minutes; this sounds strange, but it mimics the effect of a tandoori oven. Using all-purpose flour to prevent the dough from sticking, roll each dough ball out into an oblong shape that is about 12 inches on the longest side. Pull out the rack containing the stone, place the dough directly onto the pizza stone, push the rack back in, and shut the oven door. Allow each piece of naan to cook for about 2 to 3 minutes or until the top is blistered and brown. Remove the naan from the oven. Brush with garlic butter and sprinkle with chopped parsley and salt. Serve immediately. (Makes 4 pieces.)

NOTE: Special equipment: a pizza stone

ABOUT THE AUTHORS

Husband-and-wife team Justin Fox Burks and Amy Lawrence started sharing creative recipes for the home cook via The Chubby Vegetarian blog in 2008. Their popular first cookbook, *The Southern Vegetarian: 100 Down-Home Recipes for the Modern Table* (Thomas Nelson) was released in 2013. Later that year, Burks and Lawrence were invited to speak at the James Beard House in New York City for the Enlightened Eaters series; they cooked three dishes and gave a lecture on their unique style of healthy Southern cooking. Their blog, along with their expertise with vegetarian cuisine, was highlighted on *The Great Food Truck Race* on The Food Network, and Justin was the judge for the show's vegetarian challenge in Memphis. In addition, they filmed cooking segments at their home for P. Allen Smith's nationally syndicated program *Garden Style*.

Together, Justin and Amy create and photograph recipes and write articles about their passion for healthy vegetarian food. Their work and recipes have been highlighted in *The New York Times* Well blog, *The Washington Post*, *Woman's Day*, *The Kitchn*, *Local Palate*, *The Huffington Post*, *Memphis Magazine*, *Edible Memphis*, and *The Memphis Flyer*. Burks and Lawrence live in their hometown of Memphis, Tennessee with their three dogs. Outside of their time spent in the kitchen, Justin is a freelance photographer with 20 years of experience, and Amy teaches English.

@chubbyveg

The Chubby Vegetarian

thechubbyvegetarian.com

ACKNOWLEDGMENTS

Our second cookbook is here in your hands due to the direction our faith leads us and the help, support, and advice of the following folks. There are those we miss, LF Beard, Juanita Gibbs, Graham Sr. and Suzanne Burks, and Charlene and Odell Burks, and those who motivate us to do our best and to have so much fun cooking:

Susan and Chuck Schadt

Corrie Blair

Ryan Slone

Bryant Terry

P. Allen Smith

Laura Leech

Lloyd Boston

Amanda Cohen

Rich Landau

Joe Yonan

Whitney Miller

Simon Majumdar

Ermyias Shiberou of
Blue Nile Ethiopian Kitchen

Tuyen Le and Huyen Le

Krishna R. Chattu of Mayuri

Marisa Badggett

Mary "Nannie" Beard

Steve and Blandy Lawrence

Diane Lawrence, Ray Baum,
and Fleet Baum

Moishe, Lindsey, and Amelia Lettvin

The Lawrence and Fisher families

Dave, Brittany, Carson, Holden, and
Brileigh Matlock

Les, Brooke, Nathan, and Blake Mead

Virginia Maier and the Ince family

Graham Jr., Bianca, Graham III,
and Fox Burks

Hunter Burks, Keri Hutchinson,
and the Hutchinson family

Marshall, Jean Marie, Becca,
and Neely Burks

Susan Ellis

The Beard, Campbell, Stringer, and
Payan families

The Gibbs and Sellers families

Jennifer Chandler and family

The Brandstetter family

Kevin, Drue, and Scottie McCasland

Aaron, Jaimee, Charlotte,
and Catherine Cooley

The Olivere family

Aaron, Renée, Rocco, Calliope, and the
entire Brame family

Forsyth Kenworthy

Brandon and Heather Kerr

Kelly Robinson and Michael Hughes

Deni and Patrick Reilly

The Uhlhorn family

Jason and Lilly LaFerny

Jason and Meredith Nolley

Kelly English of Restaurant Iris and The
Second Line

Hannah and Amy Pickle

Ben Vaughn

Jody Moyt

Melissa and Kjeld Petersen
of *Edible Memphis*

Bianca Phillips of *Vegan Crunk*

Jill and Keith Forrester of Whitton
Farms and the Trolley Stop

Max Maloney and Marlinee Clark

Gary Backus and Margot McNeeley

Kyle and Petya Grady

Tommy Pacello and Olivia Wilmot

Stacey Greenberg

Pamela Denney

Karen Carrier of Beauty Shop, DKDC,
and Mollie Fontaine Lounge

Andrew and Emily Adams

Wally Joe of Acre and Park + Cherry

Andria Lisle

Amie Plumley

Art and Brenda Bitzer

J.C. and Danielle Youngblood

Susan and Jess Norwood

John and Wendy Rylee

Cameron and Amy Mann

David Bell

Andrew Ticer and Michael Hudman of
Andrew Michael Italian Kitchen

Felicia Willett of Felicia Suzanne's

Ryan Trimm of Sweet Grass
and Next Door

Craig and Elizabeth Blondis of
Central BBQ

Chris Wark of *Chris Beat Cancer*

Lena Wallace Black

Lee Travis

Sprouts Farmers Market and
Diego Romero

Booksellers of Laurelwood, Burke's
Books, Muddy's Bake Shop, Five-In-
One Social Club, Palladio, Cosmic
Coconut, and Babcock Gifts

The International Housewares
Association

Our friends at Contemporary Media,
Rhodes College, Shelby Farms, and
Hutchison School

And lastly, our friends on Instagram,
Twitter, and the FB...we appreciate
that you sometimes like to know what
we're having for dinner.

INDEX

www.sschadtpress.com

Published in 2016 by Susan Schadt Press
Memphis | New Orleans

© 2016 by Justin Fox Burks and Amy Lawrence

Photographs © 2016 Justin Fox Burks

Text and design © 2016 Susan Schadt Press
Designed by DOXA

Library of Congress Control Number: 2016947842

ISBN 978-0-9973559-0-1

Printed by Friesens, Altona, Canada